Also by Susan Musgrave

Poetry
Songs of the Sea-Witch
Entrance of the Celebrant
Grave-Dirt and Selected Strawberries
The Impstone
Kiskatinaw Songs
Selected Strawberries and Other Poems
Becky Swan's Book
A Man to Marry, a Man to Bury
Tarts and Muggers: Poems New and Selected 1982
Cocktails at the Mausoleum
The Embalmer's Art: Poems New and Selected 1991
Forcing the Narcissus

Fiction
The Charcoal Burners
The Dancing Chicken

Nonfiction
Great Musgrave

Children's
Gullband
Hag Head
Kestrel and Leonardo

SUSAN MUSGRAVE

MUSGRAVE LANDING

Musings on the Writing Life

Stoddart

Published in 1994 by
Stoddart Publishing Co. Limited
34 Lesmill Road
Toronto, Canada
M3B 2T6
(416) 445-3333

Canadian Cataloguing in Publication Data

Musgrave, Susan, 1951–
Musgrave landing: musings on the writing life

ISBN 0-7737-5614-0

I. Musgrave, Susan, 1951–   Anecdotes.
2. Canadian poetry (English) — History and criticism.*
3. Canadian literature (English) — History and criticism.*
I. Title.

PS8576.U74M8 1994   C811'.54   C93-095033-X
PR9199.3.M87M8 1994

Cover Concept: Angel Guerra
Cover Photograph: John Reeves
Cover Design: Brant Cowie/ArtPlus Limited
Typesetting: Tony Gordon Ltd.
Printed and bound in Canada

*Stoddart Publishing gratefully acknowledges the support of the Canada Council,
the Ontario Ministry of Culture, Tourism, and Recreation, Ontario Arts
Council, and Ontario Publishing Centre in the development of writing
and publishing in Canada.*

To Sir Richard Musgrave, bt.
Cousin Dick

Contents

PART III   *The* Susan Musgrove?

ACKNOWLEDGEMENTS

✳ My thanks to the editors of the following magazines, anthologies, and newspapers in which many of these columns first appeared: *Toronto Star, Vancouver Sun, Monday Magazine, Cut To: Magazine,* and the *Sidney Review.* A handful of the columns in this collection were also included in *Great Musgrave,* which is now out of print. "Great Expectations" appeared in *Horizons,* a high school anthology, while "Great One Goes" was first published in *The Great Big Book of Canadian Humour.*

ABOUT THE BOOK

✳ *Musgrave Landing* is a sequel to *Great Musgrave,* published by Prentice-Hall in 1989. *Great Musgrave,* which included many of the columns I'd written for the *Toronto Star* and the *Vancouver Sun,* plus other nonfiction, was nominated for the Stephen Leacock Award for Humour.

The title *Great Musgrave* doesn't stem from ego, but rather from a road sign at Great Musgrave, near Edenhall, my ancestral home on the Scottish–English border. On the back of the book there is a photo of me leaning against that sign. History, of course, is that which helps us better understand the present organization of ourselves, and when I discovered that the family motto, on my father's English side, is "We Never Change" and, on his mother's Scottish side, under a hand holding a bloody dagger, "We Make Sure," it told me more about myself than any self-help book I've ever tried. And when I learned that these border reivers — my ancestors — had carried on a three-century vendetta with a neighbouring family, it helped explain why, after three years, I had not forgiven a critic for saying, "As a title for a book, *Great Musgrave* is only a slight exaggeration."

When it came to choosing a title for a second volume, I searched for one that might again include something of my background. Two miles down the road from Great Musgrave I found, on an ordnance survey map, a Lesser Musgrave. I considered that as a possible title for this collection until I remembered the critic. Why give him a chance to say, "As a title for a book, *Lesser Musgrave* is only a slight overstatement"?

Musgrave Landing, the title of one of the columns included in this collection (about flying with my mother), was also the name given to the settlement on Saltspring Island in British Columbia where my great-grandfather built a house after emigrating from Ireland. According to a map, in 1885 the whole of the peninsula from Isabella Point to the far end of Fulford Harbour was known as the Musgrave Estate. True to their motto, the family, once again, made sure: to lose the property on the baccarat tables in Monte Carlo long before I was born to inherit it.

I wrote my biweekly column about the writing life for three years before giving it up in May 1991 so that I could get back to "my own writing" — poetry and a new novel. I meet people today, though, who claim they still read my column in the paper every week. At first I used to correct them, but I've learned now to take credit whenever I can.

One of my favourite Callahan cartoons shows a hooded man strapped into the electric chair being interviewed by a talk show host on a radio program. They are on the air, and it's a few minutes before midnight. The talk show host asks his guest, "So, where do you go from here?"

SUSAN MUSGRAVE
THE TREEHOUSE
SIDNEY, B.C.
SEPTEMBER 1993

PART I

You're Susan Muggeridge

NEVER A THOUGHT TO BEGIN WITH

✳ "Make your first sentence worthy of your death," Gordon
Lish advises writers. An editor at Knopf and the most sought-
after writing teacher in the United States, Lish claims to be able
to tell whether a manuscript is worth reading from the first three
lines. "History isn't going to give you six hundred pages to prove
you have something worth saying," Lish says. "History wants to
see your guts. Get them out there on the pavement — fast."

In many cases it's an ending that drives writers to expose their
innards (Yukio Mishima, after penning the final words in his *Sea
of Fertility* tetralogy, literally disembowelled himself). But the beginning, insists Lish, must always be a life-or-death struggle.

"What's so hard about that first sentence is that you're stuck
with it," says Joan Didion. "Everything is going to flow out of
that sentence. And by the time you've laid down the first *two* sentences, your options are all gone. The minute you start putting
words on paper you're eliminating possibilities."

But before you can even write that immortal opening, there's
the problem of getting started. How do you hook that first line?
What do you use for bait?

"You have no choice," says Annie Dillard in *The Writing Life.*
Dillard relates Ernest Thompson Seton's story of an Algonquin
woman and her baby. Left alone in their winter camp after others

had starved, the woman crawled to a lake where she found a cache containing a single fishhook. She rigged a line but had no hope of finding bait, so she took her knife and cut a strip from her own thigh, then fished with the worm of her flesh.

In every writer's life moments of personal desperation trigger beginnings. "I was facing the wall of my study," says E. L. Doctorow, "and I was so desperate to write something that I began to write about the wall. Then I wrote about the house that was attached to the wall. That's how *Ragtime* got started. . . ."

Isolation is another source of inspiration. J. P. Donleavy remembers the day he started *A Singular Man*, sitting in the sun room of a house overlooking the Atlantic in the remote west of Ireland. "One was so isolated out there . . . the local farmer came rushing across the lawn, pointing at the sky, yelling, 'There's a dog up there!' I warned my wife that the children should be pulled inside because there was a maniac loose. I was struck with terror. I had no contact with the outside world and no way of knowing the Russians had sent a dog up in a spaceship."

You're desperate, you feel isolated: what do you do next? "Get black on white" was Maupassant's advice. Another writer suggests starting with clean paper and a dirty mind. John Irving has an "enema theory": keep from writing the book as long as you can, make yourself *not begin*, store it up.

When it comes to poetry, what touches the source and ignites it? Robert Frost says: "It begins with a lump in the throat, a sense of wrong, a homesickness, a lovesickness. It is never a thought to begin with." Paul Valéry speaks of *une ligne donnée:* the first line that is a "gift" out of which you must try to pull the whole poem.

The poem in the head is always perfect, says the poet Stanley Kunitz. "Resistance starts when you try to convert it into language. Language itself is a kind of resistance to the pure flow of the self. The solution is to become one's language."

Susan Musgrave

This writer has days when the final solution is to become her punctuation — usually a series of question marks. Then it takes much more than desperation for me to get started: opening the bills helps, or reading other, more prolific writers' books.

Yesterday, for instance, before typing the first words of a short story, I flipped through the inspirational *Panati's Extraordinary Endings*. The ultimate chapter, *Final Farewells of Artists and Writers*, reminded me that history wasn't going to give me six hundred more good years to prove I had anything worth saying.

Writing a book of short stories is more difficult than writing a novel: every time you write a story you have to begin all over again, have to hook readers with a new opening line. I couldn't even use "Once upon a time," not with history clamouring for a first sentence worthy of my death.

"Why settle for less?" Mr. Lish would ask.

"THE END," I wrote finally. I always know the ending. It's a good place to start.

NOT THE WHY BUT THE WHAT

❋ So you want to be a writer? You think you know how? "All of us learn to write in the second grade. Most of us go on to greater things," said Bobby Knight, the basketball coach.

We may go on to greater things, but still we have this urge to keep writing. Hazard a guess at how many people, based on the findings of a 1988 American survey, write poetry or fiction? The answer? Forty-two million. As far as I know, no such survey has been conducted in this country, but I'm sure the figures would be just as astounding.

Few of these forty-two million will ever get published. So why do they keep writing? The Zen response to this would be "'Why?' is not a good question." It's not "why" we should be asking, but "what."

All right, then, *what* drives so many people to hit the typewriter? Jean-Jacques Rousseau claimed that writing becomes necessary when speech fails to protect our identity. The written word may be, for some, a weak second-best to lived experience, but for others it is one of the most powerful ways of transforming experience.

Often we use writing to get attention or love. James Jones felt the quality that makes a person want to write and be read is essentially a desire for self-exposure and is masochistic.

Which brings us to sex. To get a woman, all a man has to do is say he's a writer; it's an aphrodisiac, according to Saul Bellow, although my experience with the opposite sex has been the opposite. If *I* say I'm a writer, more often I get, "Could you introduce me to your publisher? I'm working on a book . . ."

Some write for reasons of vanity, from a desire for celebrity or immortality. George Orwell was only being honest when he said his leading motive was the desire to be thought clever, to be talked about by people he'd never met.

Writing, for a great number of people, has a therapeutic effect. It's never a total cure — much happens in life from which there is no recovery — but if you stay drunk on writing, reality will never completely destroy you. You can't cure grief or death, but you can do your best to oppose it, creatively.

"Why urge everybody to write when the world is so full of writers?" asks Brenda Ueland. Ueland's experience has taught her that "everybody is talented, original, and has something important to say." "And if (as I wish) everybody writes and respects and loves writing, then we would have a nation of intelligent, eager, impassioned readers."

Would that that were so. *My* experience has been that too many people think they can write a book without having read one. Reasons for not reading range from "don't have enough time" to — the lamest of all — fear of "being influenced." Professional writers, who often spend a great deal of their time reading, get cranky when they hear these excuses.

Susan Musgrave

"Everywhere I go I'm asked if I think the university stifles writers," said Flannery O'Connor. "My opinion is that they don't stifle enough of them."

But creative writing classes can't be blamed for this universal writing fever. The reasons go back to grade two when we first learned to write. By the time we leave high school most of us can write well — at least well enough to fill in an unemployment insurance application form when we have to — and many get the impression that anyone can crank out a book. At a party in Ottawa, after being introduced to a former Cabinet minister, he said to me, "That's one thing I haven't tried yet — writing a book." It's as though one only had to *try* and one would become a writer.

Writing is a whole lifetime and a lot of practice. It takes years to write a book. Of course, there are aberrations like William Faulkner, who claimed to have knocked off *As I Lay Dying* in six weeks during time off from a full-time labouring job. And there are other examples, just as there are those who swallow swords, camp on flagpoles, dive off cliffs, or have themselves buried alive. But, "Out of a human population of four and a half billion, perhaps twenty people can write a book in a year," Annie Dillard says. "There is no call to take human extremes as norm."

Still, sometimes it seems as if everyone must be an author. "When I retire, I'm going to write a book," the neurosurgeon informs Margaret Atwood at a literary gathering. "When I retire," Atwood replies, "I'm going to become a brain surgeon."

TOOLS OF THE TRADE

❈ Writers get touchy about their equipment. John Steinbeck's pencils had to be round (hexagonal ones cut his fingers after a long day); Thomas Fuller preferred a peacock's quill "because its

Feathers are all Eyes." Others swear a magical pen is the symbol and the tool of the real writer.

Many writers complete their first drafts in longhand because handwriting is more connected to the movement of the heart. In typing, where the fingers hit keys and pages are filled with straight bold lines of uniform black letters, a different aspect of yourself may surface.

John Barth says he finds typing — where each letter is physically separated by a little space from the next letter — a paralyzing notion. "Good old script," he says, "which connects this letter to that, and this line to that — well, that's how good plot works, right?"

There are good reasons why some writers, like Isaac Asimov, should stick with their Sheaffers. Asimov recalls sitting in front of his new word processor — a gift from the Tandy Corporation — to begin work on his four hundredth book. When he switched the machine on, nothing happened. Not daring to tinker with it, he dialled 911.

The dispatcher suggested he call Radio Shack, where the salesperson said he would have to purchase a service contract before a repairman could be sent. Asimov raced to town, wrote a cheque for $1,402, then returned home to wait it out.

In the time it took the repairman to arrive, Asimov could have handwritten two novels. The repairman glanced at the machine, then strolled over to the wall switch and flicked it on. The machine began to hum, and a friendly greeting flashed across the screen. Asimov got a bill for $89.

Where I live repairmen don't make house calls. So last week when my computer developed a glitch I had to lug it to town and entrust it to a stranger who said he might or might not have time to look at it before the long weekend, and then recommended a nearly new laptop model in "the $10,000 range."

On the way home, shopping for my daughter's grade three school supplies, I was reminded of how simple life used to be when my only question was how did they get the lead into the middle of an HB pencil? In those days my memory was in my hands; on the third finger of my right hand I developed a callus from gripping the pencil. Now I spend my days at a machine whose owner's manuals weigh more than the antique Remington I learned to type on. My entire literary oeuvre is stored in a memory bank thinner than my chewed-down baby fingernail.

I have to remind myself why I traded in my Remington — because I liked the way a printer returns the carriage automatically. Now I can write nonstop without having to worry about my thoughts being jarred by the typewriter alarm bell going off at the end of each line. I can write, that is, when my machine isn't in the shop or my nose in an operator's manual.

The long weekend comes and goes and when, on Tuesday, I phone the repairshop, the owner thinks he *should* be able to have a look at it by Friday. He's afraid it's going to need a new part, one that went out with the peacock's quill, but he's still open for offers on that reconditioned laptop.

I chew what's left of my fingernails, realizing how spoiled I've become. What about all the writers who never even possessed an HB pencil stub? They still found ways to leave their mark, writing epics in blood, inscribing diaries on cigarette papers, and carving immortal poems in bars of soap. Lady Jane Grey, awaiting execution in the Tower of London, composed verses on scraps of paper using tiny pinpricks, which were discovered later when held to the light.

In the bottom drawer of my filing cabinet, in a boxful of mementos, I dig out the magical fountain pen I bought with my first royalty cheque. Back then I believed the pen was mightier than the sword until I tried to dispatch a couple of literary critics with my gold-nibbed Parker. Now, having spent an afternoon taking my Parker apart, I learn another lesson. The sword is easier to clean, too.

I'm about to leave a suicide note in saliva when my daughter comes to show off her well-sharpened pencils and offers to lend me one. My heart skips a beat: I grip the pencil — it fits snugly into the callus I never lost. I go to work. I have more to say than ever before now that I lack the technology.

THE TITLE YOU GO WITH

❋ A French publisher with a macabre sense of humour produced an edition of Rousseau's *The Social Contract* bound in the skins of aristocrats guillotined during the French Revolution. This may be one exception to the adage, "you can't know a book by its cover," but how much can you tell about a book from its title?

Critics seldom miss a chance to *judge* a book by its title. "*Howl* (by Allen Ginsberg) is meant to be a noun, but I can't help taking it as an imperative," wrote John Hollander in the *Partisan Review*. When a young poet sent editor Eugene Field a tedious manuscript entitled *Why Do I Live?* Field wrote on the rejection slip, "Because you send your poem by mail."

"Beauty is truth, truth beauty — that is all / Ye know on earth and all ye need to know," wrote John Keats in "Ode on a Grecian Urn." In truth, the poet used poetic licence in titling his poem: the vase that inspired Keats was a Wedgwood copy of a Roman copy of a Greek vase. The poem would more accurately have been titled "Ode on a Doubly Fake Grecian Urn."

"Poets have been mysteriously silent on the subject of cheese," said G. K. Chesterton, which may have prompted Michael Ondaatje to consider *The Cheese Stands Alone* as a working title for his collection of poems, *Secular Love*. Ondaatje made a wise change; *The Cheese Stands Alone* could have landed in some bookstores' Cookery section like another of his poetry titles, *There's a Trick with a Knife I'm Learning to Do*.

Working titles often change. The year *Mila 18*, Leon Uris's bestselling novel, was due to be published by Doubleday, Simon and Schuster announced they, too, had a novel with the number eighteen in the title. Joseph Heller agreed, eventually, to rename his book, and *Catch-18* became *Catch-22*.

Anne Sexton gave up more than just a title to save her marriage; she cut her poem. "As I was writing 'Twenty-One Days Without You,' my husband said to me, 'I can't stand it any longer. You haven't been with me for days.'" Sexton's poem became "Eighteen Days Without You."

But some writers refuse to change. For one of its main selections in 1951 the Book-of-the-Month Club chose *The Catcher in the Rye*, but the editors felt the title was too obscure. When they asked the author if he would consider a different one, J. D. Salinger wrote back, "Holden Caulfield wouldn't like that."

"Getting a title is a lot like drawing cards in a poker game," Ernest Hemingway said. "You keep on drawing but if you can last at it long enough you always get a good hand finally."

Even when the author gets the right title, finally, there are others who get it wrong. "Do you stock *Anne of Clarke Gables?*" a bookshop owner in Halifax got asked. An order emanating from Palestine for T. E. Lawrence's *Seven Pillars of Wisdom* produced a happy error in transmission: the sought-after title became *Seven Kilos of Wisdom*.

In 1982 a group of booksellers invited me to co-judge a book title contest. A magnum of champagne would be awarded to the publisher who submitted the name of the most improbable title on offer at an international book fair. *Nuclear War Fun Book* — an activity book to amuse children after the big bang has disrupted their favourite television programs — was my personal favourite, but my fellow judge wanted to split the magnum between the publishers of *Tourists' Guide to Lebanon* and *The Creation* (revised edition). In the end we chose *Big and Very Big Hole Drilling* from the Technical Publishing House in Bucharest — the very last title on both our lists.

"A good title comes last," Tennessee Williams said, although in a different context. He admits that *Blanche's Chair in the Moon*, the working title he gave to one of his plays, was a bad choice, but it was from that image, of a woman sitting by a window, that *A Streetcar Named Desire* came to him.

The title always comes first to me and, as my editor reminds me, to the reader. Desire, she says, is one of three key ingredients. A good title has sex in it, power, and travel.

I've never had trouble coming up with titles; where I do get into trouble is crossing international borders with copies of my books: *A Man to Marry, a Man to Bury; Grave-Dirt; Cocktails at the Mausoleum.* I've never met a customs officer yet who doesn't think he can tell everything about me from the titles of my books.

EDITOR, EDITOR

✳ "No passion in the world is equal to the passion to alter someone else's draft," said H. G. Wells. But when Oscar Wilde was asked to make changes in one of his plays, he refused. "Who am I to tamper with a masterpiece?" he protested.

Patrick Hemingway once asked his father to edit a short story he'd written. Hemingway read the manuscript twice, then returned it to his son. "But, Papa," Patrick cried, "you've only changed one word!"

"If it's the right word," said Hemingway, "that's the lot."

Every author needs an editor, although often the relationship is knife-to-throat. "Cut these words and they would bleed" was Emerson's response on being asked to delete a couple of copulative verbs his editor didn't like.

Eugene O'Neill, too, resisted altering his drafts. When a director requested that he shorten his play, *Ah, Wilderness!* by fifteen minutes, O'Neill cut the third intermission.

O'Neill, employed as a news reporter on the *New London Tele-*

graph, also found it difficult to please newspaper editors. One contribution was returned to him with the following note: "This is a lovely story, but would you mind finding out the name of the gentleman who carved the lady and whether the dame is his wife or daughter or who? And phone the hospital for a hint as to whether she is dead or discharged or what? Then put the facts into a hundred and fifty words and send this literary batik to the picture framers."

But even when it isn't knife-to-throat, an author-editor relationship is an intimate one. After Goethe's confession, in a new edition of his autobiography, "With this woman, for the first time, I really fell in love," a scholarly editor added an asterisk and the information, "Here Goethe was in error."

For other writers, like Thomas Wolfe, the author-editor relationship is a marriage of sorts. Wolfe, who demanded round-the-clock attention from his editor, Maxwell Perkins, lived and slept in Perkins's office. One of the most sought-after editors of all time, Perkins (who warned that "editors are extremely fallible people, all of them. Don't put too much trust in them.") nearly lost his job at Scribner's because other authors resented the excessive attention Wolfe was getting.

When Thomas Wolfe dedicated his first lengthy novel to Perkins, a copy was sent to F. Scott Fitzgerald for his views. "Dear Max," ran Fitzgerald's reply. "I liked the dedication, but after that I thought it fell off a bit." Fitzgerald, who described himself as more of a "taker-outer" than Wolfe (a "putter-inner"), would have cut the manuscript in half.

Perkins kept his job, although ultimately it was Wolfe who left, feeling betrayed. In a paranoid state of mind Wolfe conceived the idea that Perkins had "tamed" his books by playing so large a part in editing them.

Wolfe's paranoia supports the widely held belief about editors — that they are really just failed writers. When T. S. Eliot's editor asked him what *he* believed, Eliot pondered for a moment, then said, "I suppose some editors are failed writers — but so are most writers."

John Cheever had his own special definition of a good editor: "A man I think charming, who gives me large cheques, praises my work, my physical beauty, and my sexual prowess, and who has a stranglehold on the bank."

A slightly edited version of Cheever's definition (stet "stranglehold on the bank") would describe my own editor, who is also my husband. He's a passionate deletionist. But no passion in the world is equal to the passion a putter-inner feels when a taker-outer takes his blunt pencil to her polished draft.

I never show my husband a new poem until I'm sure it's word-perfect. "This won't need work," I tell him. My husband, at first, is charming. He praises my attempts so far, then tells me not to change a word of my title. After that his enthusiasm drops off. His "it doesn't need *much* work" is like the dentist's "it won't hurt a bit."

Work always hurts. If, on the other hand, he ever said, "Don't tamper with it. It's a masterpiece," I would probably rewrite every stanza, *and* the title.

As Oscar Wilde put it, "When editors agree with me, I feel I *must* be wrong."

THE EXPRESSION OF SOMETHING REAL

❉ There's the story of the Zen poet who hiked to a mountaintop where he meditated, in search of truth. After thirty-nine years, he hiked down from the mountain. The truth was, he said, he'd wasted his time.

The thirty-nine hours I'd wasted on research seemed like small beer in comparison, but now I had a newspaper editorial writer on the line. I argued that my essay "Everything I Write Is a Lie" was, in fact, a dissertation on truth.

"A writer is congenitally unable to tell the truth," said William Faulkner, "and that is why we call what he writes *fiction*. My fiction had landed me the job of writing a "Worry-of-the-Week" essay for the editorial page of a local weekly giveaway. I'd cut my journalistic molars on a piece about Huggies destroying the Earth, and now I wanted something I could really sink my fangs into.

"The truth is not facts," I said to the editorial writer. "It's the expression of something *real.*"

"Then why don't you write about the abortion issue?" he suggested patiently. "No one wants 'truth' on the editorial page."

Thomas Jefferson once said that advertisements contain the only truths to be relied on in a newspaper. "I was hoping to be humorous," I added.

"Hey, don't let me discourage you," the editorial writer said, and then explained to me how humour worked. "Say you're writing about inflation. You might say, 'Inflation is getting terrible. I went to the supermarket today and put a down payment on a leg of lamb.'"

I waited until he had control of himself again before I asked how many inches he wanted on the abortion issue.

There was a pause. "Okay," he said finally. "You're right. Everyone's doing abortions." He gave me a list of alternatives. Whatever you do, *tell* the truth, promise me. Just don't write about it," he said.

I took his advice and switched to the topic furthest from the truth as possible — politics. It was worrying, I began, that our former premier had gone to bed every night in a castle. It was worrying, I concluded, that the amount of government funding for the arts in British Columbia last year equalled the cost of paving four feet of the Coquihalla Highway.

It was also worrying that in revealing too much, my essay might get edited. But, as Rita Mae Brown says, "If people refrain from telling what they know, how long before they actively lie?

Is there not a subtle and corrosive connection between withholding the truth and lying?"

I faxed my "Worry-of-the-Week" to the paper, and waited. While waiting I prepared to defend my position ("Every government is run by liars and nothing they say should be believed." — I. F. Stone) and my technique ("Get your facts first, then distort them as you please." — Mark Twain). I believed that my essay, now retitled "Everything They Say Is a Lie," would put the newspaper's name in the headlines. All I had left to do was convince the newspaper.

Chairman Mao, who also hiked in China (as opposed to his successors who rolled through Tiananmen Square), said you can judge your success by the reaction against you. When the editorial writer finally called, it wasn't to offer me a new position as political commentator. He'd talked it over with "his leader," and they both felt there was a place for me on the entertainment page. There I'd be able to express myself more freely.

In the act of reviewing *Oral Sadism and the Vegetarian Personality* for the book corner of the entertainment page, I discovered I would be expressing myself more freely if I went to the nearest mountaintop and took a vow of silence for the rest of my life. Still, I was a professional, and I finished saying all there was to be said about oral sadism before phoning the editorial writer.

I was thirty-nine years old, I told him. I didn't have time to review *When You Have Chest Pains: A Guide to Cardiac and Noncardiac Causes* before next week. But quicker than I could have said "I quit," he had offered me a permanent job, one with "tonnes of growth potential, a competitive salary, and health benefits" — writing advertising copy.

Someone said all newspaper editorial writers ever do is come down from the hills after the battle is over and shoot the wounded.

Ain't it the truth.

Susan Musgrave

BECAUSE IT ISN'T THERE

✳ Stephen King is sitting in a café around the corner from his house, grabbing a little lunch by himself and reading a book. A customer sidles up to him and asks, "Why aren't you reading one of your *own* books?"

"I know how they all come out," says King, and returns to his hamburger.

In the minds of readers, he says, writers exist to serve two purposes, and the more important may not be the writing. The primary function of writers, it seems, is to answer readers' questions.

King says these fall into three categories. There are the "One-of-a-Kind Questions" that often reflect the writer's field of interest. The bearded King has been asked everything from "Are you morbid of razors?" to "Ever et raw meat?"

Then there are the Old Standards, such as "Where do you get your ideas?" (in Utica, he says), and finally, the "Real Weirdies" — questions like, "Writing any good books lately?" Through the process of elimination (he's discarded about five hundred other possibilities) King has developed an answer: "I'm taking some time off."

Having an answer is a good thing, he says, but it doesn't solve the problem of *what the question means.* "It is this inability on my part to make sense of this odd query, which reminds me of that Zen riddle — 'Why is a mouse when it runs?' — that leaves me feeling mentally shaken and impotent." It isn't just one question, he says, it's a *bundle* of questions, cunningly wrapped up in one package.

King, the self-described "McDonald's of literature," is constantly recognized in public. But for the majority of writers, by far the most difficult question is, "What do *you* do?" "If you were a member of Jesse James' band and people asked you what you were, you wouldn't say, 'Well, I'm a desperado,'" writes Roy Blount, Jr. "You'd say something like 'I work in banks' or 'I've done some railroad work.' It took me a long time just to say 'I'm a writer.' It's really embarrassing."

"What do you do?" is quickly followed by other loaded questions, such as "Should I know your name?" or "What have you written that I might have read?" Most of the time, though, people ask questions that describe their own predicament ("Do you ever find you run out of ideas?") or questions to which there *are* no real answers. "What is truth?" asks one inquisitor after a poetry reading. The truth is, no one likes questions that have no real answers.

So, out of pure necessity, I've developed my own repertoire of responses. Actually, it's a repertoire of *other* people's answers, for as Peter Anderson has said, "Stealing someone else's words frequently spares the embarrassment of eating one's own."

I've a One-of-a-Kind Answer — S. J. Perelman-style — for the radio interviewer asking how many drafts I do. "Thirty-seven. I once tried doing thirty-three, but something was lacking. On another occasion I tried forty-two versions, but the final effect was too lapidary — you know what I mean, Jack?" I've an Old Standard for reporters who ask why I switched to journalism ("Truth is shorter than fiction." — Irving Cohen) and a Real Weirdie for talk show hosts who want to know why I write ("Because it isn't there." — Thomas Berger.)

No one resents questions from people who honestly want answers. Recently I went to price a new car, and the salesman, who remembered me composing poetry in grade ten biology, eyed the ancient Beetle I was driving and asked, "How's the writing going?" It wasn't just one question; it was a whole bundle. If it was going where *he* thought it ought to have gone by now, I'd be driving a BMW, fully loaded.

Sometimes I'm tempted to give an honest answer — the doubt; the deadlines; the conflicts, crises, and unresolved resolutions; the search for themes; the Bad Sector on the computer; the printer refusing, intermittently, to double-space; the unpaid-off advances; the expenses; an editor's passion to alter your draft — but, then again, does anybody really want to know?

"Why is a Beetle when it keeps running?" I cry as I flee the showroom. But I can't get out the door — I always push where I am supposed to pull — and the salesman has to open it for me. Unshaken, he suggests, "Why don't you take some time off . . . ?"

THE RIGHT AMOUNT OF FAME

"Fame lost its appeal for me when I went into a public rest room and an autograph-seeker handed me a pen and paper under the stall door," said Marlo Thomas.

Most writers don't get that famous. According to Fran Lebowitz, writers get *exactly* the right amount of fame — enough to get a good table in a restaurant but not so much that people are constantly interrupting you while you're eating dinner.

Although the interruptions may not be constant, some writers do get the odd one. Truman Capote was sitting in a crowded Key West bar one night when a mildly drunk woman came over and asked him to sign her paper napkin. This upset her very drunk husband, who staggered over and unzipped his pants. "Since you're autographing things, why don't you autograph this?" he said.

"I don't know if I can autograph it," Capote replied after giving it the once-over, "but perhaps I can *initial* it."

W. P. Kinsella was spotted in a Chinese restaurant in North Carolina. After he read the menu, a Chinese gentleman approached him. W.P. ordered chicken fried rice and the almond chop suey. "Mr. Kinsella, sir?" the man asked. W.P. was astonished that anyone that far south would recognize him. "I was at your reading this afternoon and enjoyed it very much," the man continued. Then he returned to his own table where he was having dinner with his wife.

One amazing product of fame, should it come to you, says Rita Mae Brown, is the number of people claiming to know you. Everyone from your grandmother to the shoe salesman at K Mart will accuse you of having trampled over them on your ruthless climb to the top. Strangers will swear to past nights of physical bliss, and if you don't pay them off, they'll go to the *National Enquirer*. You will be plagued by clairvoyants who have the secrets to your future.

It hasn't reached the stage where I have to wear a false nose and glasses whenever I go to the Laundromat, but after appearing on TV recently as a book panelist, I do get the odd person claiming to know me.

The other night, for example, my husband and I went to a local restaurant. We got a table for two next to the His and Hers (no maître d' I've ever known has been impressed by literature), and during our appetizer, a woman across the room kept staring at me. "I know *her*," I heard her repeating all through our entrée. She kept on drinking until we finished dessert, when she lurched up to our table and proclaimed, the room having grown silent, "I know you. You're Susan Muggeridge."

Mostly we eat at home, although even there I get the occasional interruption. "It's for you," says my husband as I pour the wine and clear a space on the table for the soufflé. He holds the telephone at arm's length. He has that "I told you we should get an unlisted phone number" look in his eyes.

"Is this Susan Musgrave, the writer?" queries a voice. "We had the same English teacher once and my boyfriend was in your math class, so I bought your book," she confesses. "The one with cannibals in it. I thought it was really cute."

Cute wasn't what I'd had in mind.

"I've never known any famous authors before," my caller continues, "but my boyfriend says I should meet you and tell you about *my* life."

Like Evelyn Waugh, I don't believe the expenditure of $4.95

for a book entitles the purchaser to the personal friendship of the author. I wave my husband into the kitchen to rescue the soufflé — it smells done — and remind my caller of what Mark Twain said, that "Fame is a vapour; popularity an accident; the only earthly certainty is oblivion."

"That's one way of putting it. Some days I drink too much, that's for sure," she responds, "but even when I'm sober I think your work is pretty good. I hope you never stop writing."

The fruit flies in my wine are getting woozier by the moment. I think of Robert Benchley saying it took him fifteen years to discover he had no talent for writing but he couldn't give it up because by that time he was too famous.

Only when my caller "has to run" do I sit down to my soufflé, which is definitely done-for. I sieve a few fruit flies through my teeth and knock the wine back.

"The only earthly certainty is oblivion," my husband echoes, reaching to refill my glass.

A WINDOW ONTO THE REAL WORLD

✵ Mail is an occupational hazard of the writer's life. A day doesn't pass without the mailbox getting clogged with requests for favours. The Don't Sigh, Eat Pie Restaurant wants me to re-write their menu. A literary fund-raiser desires my underwear for an auction.

"I know you may be surprised to receive a letter from a stranger especially when you are least expecting it," begins the third letter I slit open. I skip the parts commending me on my integrity and cut to the point of the letter.

The stranger wants me to recommend him for a grant. I file his request under "To Be Answered Immediately." Some of this correspondence dates back to 1955.

"I am doing an independent study unit on an unknown

Canadian writer," writes my next correspondent, a grade thirteen student from Happy Valley High. "I would like to know what some of the joys and problems you face as an aspiring writer are." After that comes an invitation to play a nude nurse in *The Maternity Ward* at the Fringe Festival.

"By now you know you are dealing with a real wacko," a regular from Calgary writes in his seventh missive of the week. "What primary characteristic do you think all writers should possess?" Self-preservation. For this reason I never write back.

Writers have different ways of dealing with unwanted mail. John Milton went blind to avoid having to read any more unsolicited manuscripts, and Edmund Wilson had postcards printed up that read, "Edmund Wilson regrets that it is impossible for him to . . ." followed by a long list of things he did not do — which included just about everything — with the appropriate one checked off. His idea backfired, though, because people started writing to him just to get one of his famous cards.

For John Gregory Dunne the wackos and the strangers are a constant of the daily post. Since he's a public figure, his private life gets scrutinized. "You still have not taken my advice and dumped that miserable piece of New York Jewish dreck you are married to," one fan writes, berating him every time Dunne — whose wife, the writer Joan Didion, is a WASP from Sacramento — publishes a piece. Another well-wisher listed Dunne's house in the Sunday real estate section of the *Los Angeles Times*: "Famous writer's loss is your gain. Brentwood Park's finest two-storey mansion completely redone . . ." at two-thirds of market value. Dunne went hoarse trying to convince buyers the ad was a joke.

But, he says, wackos are important to a writer, "because most of us have a professional interest in aberrant behaviour." The wacko who insults your spouse or puts a house up for sale opens a window onto the "real" world. Writers, too, are always on the lookout for new perspectives, so that someone like Eddie, whose return address reads, "State Prison of Southern Michigan. World's Largest Walled Prison. Better known as the Walled-Off Astoria," holds an irresistible attraction for Dunne.

The remainder of today's mail stares up at me, like a dare. I file the request for underwear under "To Be Answered Eventually" and open the next letter bomb. "I hope you will reply one of these centuries," perseveres my Calgary correspondent in letter number eight, "although eternal hope has utterly betrayed me in the past."

I'm running out of hope myself (the cheques I'm waiting for aren't in the mail) when the return address on the last letter in the pile hooks my eye: "U. R. A. Millionaire," from a box number in Kingston.

I stab myself breaking into the jiffy bag that has been sealed with twenty staples instead of the requisite five. Alas, U. R. A. Millionaire is not the patron I've been waiting for, but one of many aliases used by a con in the Kingston Pen doing twenty years for extortion. He admits he's never read any of my "attempts at poetry, but from what I've seen on one or two TV clips, your visage is quite arresting, with crooked teeth interesting in the extreme."

The old "buttering me up for the I have a favour to extort from you" routine. I skip ahead to find out what he really wants — an autographed volume maybe, a pen pal perhaps, but more than likely a money order.

As fate would have it, U. R. A. Millionaire is writing his memoirs, and if I can fix it with a publisher, he'll put me in touch with an underworld orthodontist in Philadelphia who'll fix *me*.

It's one favour I can't refuse.

✳ "Writing was always an obsession with me," said Truman Capote. "It was as if I were an oyster and somebody forced a grain of sand into my shell. . . ." Even though a pearl would form around that grain and irritate him, make him angry, the oyster couldn't "help becoming obsessed with the pearl."

Writers usually end up writing about their obsessions. They write about what haunts them, keeps them awake at night. Natalie Goldberg, who teaches a Zen approach to writing, tells her students to make lists of their obsessions so that they can see what they unconsciously (and consciously) spend their waking hours thinking about. This gives them plenty to write about.

Your main obsessions have power, says Goldberg in *Writing Down the Bones*. They usually take over your life whether you want them to or not, so you might as well make them work for you.

I sit down to make a list. The most I get obsessed about these days is defrosting the refrigerator; my list is still blank when the new dog next door starts barking.

"It's the height of rudeness to move into a neighbourhood and put your dog out to bark," I complain to my husband, who is lost in his newspaper on the back porch in the sun. "Who's barking?" He flips to the entertainment section. "I didn't hear barking — until you arrived."

The new neighbours are deliberately trying to ruin my concentration, I tell him. Sensitive people would lock a dog up. What did they plan to do — let him bark all night? People like that shouldn't be allowed to own dogs. They probably moved here because there's no bylaw covering dog droppings, and next I'll have to wear plastic bags over my shoes when I walk across our lawn.

"They moved in yesterday," says my husband. "Give the dog a chance to adjust." His look accuses me of searching for something to get obsessed about because my life has become too quiet.

Susan Musgrave

That's *all* I want, I tell him as the barking crescendos into a howl. A quiet life so I can write.

Now there's an obsession to begin my list with: writing. For years critics have said my poetry is preoccupied with death, but Freud says an obsession with death is nothing more than a healthy obsession with life. In the meantime I recall one that is more immediate, and add to my list "the new carpet."

"Women are afraid of their demon, want to control it, make it sensible like themselves," says the protagonist in one of May Sarton's novels. It is my husband's view that my need to control who walks over my new carpet, and when, is not sensible at all, but has to do with the fact that I am wrestling with my own demons. I haven't finished a poem since the carpet was installed.

Yesterday I had it professionally cleaned. When the rug doctor asked if I wanted my carpet protected, my husband began to laugh. He feels I have been *overly protective* toward the carpet — I asked him to walk around it. When he pointed out that you can't walk around a wall-to-wall carpet, I thought I solved the problem by laying an outlaw trail of old newspapers. This prompted my husband to show me a letter in one of the papers from "Raked but Not Ruined," whose mother was so obsessed she not only vacuumed the rug every day, she raked it. If you made the mistake of walking into the living room, you had to rake your way back out.

Obsession. The story of my life — as Capote would have it — in an oyster shell. Now the new dog has stopped barking, so there is peace and I can return to my office. But the silence is almost a kind of noise in itself and, unable to bear it, I break for an early lunch.

It's Friday, the day I defrost, so I scramble some partially thawed spaghetti sauce together with a bit of old codfish in the frying pan. My husband, drawn to the kitchen, sniffs. "Poisoning the dog is not going to put us on good terms with the neighbours."

Edna Ferber wrote that in order to write really convincingly, one must be somewhat poisoned by emotion. "Dislike, displeasure, resentment, fault-finding, obsession, passionate remonstrance, a sense of injustice — they all make fine fuel."

I eat lunch in my office and begin writing obsessively. "Poisoning the neighbours was not going to put us on good terms with the dog. . . ."

A DARING ADVENTURE OR NOTHING

❋ Don't get yourself in a nice, safe, comfortable situation where you're afraid or unable to take risks is Tom Robbins's advice to young writers. Serious writers, he says, take risks.

For some writers a nice, safe, comfortable situation is risky enough. Take the risk of getting out of bed in the morning. If I'm to believe *Ripley's Believe It or Not*, beds caused 77,581 injuries last year and pillows another 445.

So even before I toss the comforter back, I reach for the bedside light. According to *Ripley's*, this could be my first (and last) mistake of the day. Faulty wiring extinguishes 500 people annually.

Having made it into my dressing gown without bodily harm or electrocution, I hesitate outside the bathroom. I'm about to enter a room where more people drown in bathtubs than in any other room of the house. But life is either a daring adventure or nothing, so I steel my nerves to get through the door. One out of every 360 families suffers a door-related injury.

During breakfast, I read the list of ingredients on my box of Natural Life cereal as I listen to the CBC for news of today's carcinogen. It's Saturday, and "the greatest risk of cancer is from natural elements in food itself."

I scrape my breakfast into our toxic wastebasket and flip the switch on the main power breaker; it's my husband's turn to guard the baby. After barricading the stairs, the food cupboards, and the bathroom, I clothe her in Flame Retardant Material Only and head for the university library.

Driving on the highway is by far the biggest risk. One in four Canadians has been injured in a car accident. Mondays and Tuesdays are the safest days on the road, but if you're driving on Saturday, it's most important to wear clean underwear.

Today I'm one of the chosen ones who reaches her destination. I choose my books and hand the librarian my Fee-Paying Extramural Borrowing Card. The librarian looks flustered; she can't remember which of the two date-stamps she's supposed to use. Finally she makes a "wild guess" and picks the one closest to hand. "What would life be without risk?" she sighs.

I tell her she's risking her life just *being* at work, that millions of disabling accidents occur in the workplace every year. She could be hit by a falling object or contract asbestosis in the time it takes her to stamp my books "Due Back Tuesday."

Once more there's the parking lot to reconnoitre. But even if I do reach my car (the odds of my being run over by a bus are as good as my chances of appearing on *The Tonight Show*, 1 in 490,000), there's the drive home. It's still early — prime accident time is between 10:00 p.m. and 2:00 a.m. — but it's raining, so I brake at every green light I hit. Near the airport I brake for a hitchhiker, my sodden next-door neighbour's son. I never pick up strangers these days unless I recognize them — it's too risky. Inevitably they ask, "Mind if I smoke?"

The number of premature deaths due to smoking is the equivalent of 920 fully loaded 747 jumbo jets crashing every year. One is coming in for a landing right now as my neighbour's son reaches into his knapsack for a carton of Lucky Strikes.

"It's not that I mind smoke," I assure him, rolling down my window as he strikes his first match. "The fresh air will do me good." At least I hope it will do me good. Air pollution, I have to remind myself, took 20,000 lives last year in the east.

I drop my neighbour's son outside the tobacconist's where I begrudgingly purchase my husband's lottery ticket. It's not the expenditure of a hard-earned loonie (he reimburses me) that bothers me; in my books the chance of winning more money than I'd need to pay off my Visa bill is the biggest risk of all.

That night, when the Fisher-Price Room Monitor is switched on over the baby's crib (forty-four percent of crib deaths have been prevented by such devices), I unplug the television set, the toaster, and every other lightning conductor in the house. Then it's bed — somewhere safe and comfortable to collapse at the end of the day. Or maybe not; most people, after all, die in bed.

I extinguish the light and crawl in beside my husband, who is already dreaming of this week's Lotto 6/49. His chances of winning with a single ticket? One in five million.

It's not a chance *I'd* take. I can't afford to get myself in a nice, safe, comfortable financial situation where I'm unwilling to take the kinds of risks *serious* writers take.

WAITING FOR THE LIBRARIANS

❋ Most writers will sell their souls, and other parts, too, if it buys them time. Brian Patten, the English poet, writes about being trapped in the bowels of Cornell University where, between rows of mildewed manuscripts, he comes across the more recent acquisitions. Robert Lowell's left eye still blinks in serious astonishment, Auden's tarry lungs wheeze on in exasperation next to the decomposed kidneys of Dylan Thomas, which had been smuggled at great expense from a New York morgue. "Thus does poetry survive in Academia," Patten writes.

Survival at the most basic level is often what makes poets part with their literary remains. Allen Ginsberg claims he sells his archive by the pound. He even includes his grocery lists.

I had never been tempted to sell my papers. The idea of some nosey parker picking through my wastepaper basket to support his thesis seemed like an invasion. But when a dealer called and explained how my work sheets would cast light upon the creative process for future students of literature, he almost seduced me. And when he said he could get more money for my rough drafts than I'd made from all my books of poetry over the years, I surrendered.

It took a bit of getting used to — the idea of making money. I was still thinking of ways to squander my fortune when the dealer called back. He had made the librarians an offer they would jump at right away if I threw in — along with my work sheets — press clippings, profiles, and any revealing photographs.

I was reluctant to sell some of these. On the other hand I didn't want to end up like the aging actress I'd read about, who'd been found smothered to death by a collection of her personal press clippings. I blew the cobwebs off my own personal press clippings and sent them along to the dealer.

The dealer came to meet me and stepped up his original offer. When I balked at selling my correspondence from friends and business associates, he assured me the letters were less likely to be read once they were entombed in the library vaults than if they remained in my own filing cabinets. I eventually broke down and gave him my journals under a controlled-access clause. Students of literature would, fifty years after my death, be privy to some of the best-kept literary scandals of our time, and in the interim I could afford to hook up to the neighbourhood sewer. There would even be money left over, which would buy me time to write.

We were still waiting for a decision from the librarians. The dealer went through my drawers and said we could make my archive even more attractive by offering my personal correspondence files.

When it came to selling my love letters, I had serious reservations. What were the rules and limitations imposed by custom and good taste? Was it prudent to sell a dead love's letters while he still reviewed weekly for the *Globe and Mail?*

When an engagement is broken, the rules say that love letters must be returned to the writer. When a love affair with a writer ends, I learned, anything goes . . . to the highest bidder. The dealer gave me an example of a minor poet who sold the love letters he'd received from a major poet in less time than it took Roy Orbison to sing "It's Over."

"There is nothing deader than a dead love letter," the dealer said, poring over my files, "unless it's a carbon copy of a dead love letter." He pointed out that I'd written the same love letter, the same day, to two different men. I couldn't remember being in love with either of them, but I was willing to sell both carbons so that students of literature might have light cast upon the creative process in the future.

Twenty years of my life were chronicled in the cancelled cheque and dinner-party menus I itemized for Special Collections. I scraped together lists of first-aid items to be taken on camping trips and Post-its with scraps of poetry inspired at the Laundromat while waiting for the spin cycle to finish. Waiting for the librarians to phone and give me their verdict, I thought of Robert Lowell's left eye blinking on in the pristine catacombs of Cornell. I could go one step further.

I could offer both eyes, or my heart, under a controlled-access clause. For a lump sum I would have my whole body wrapped in work sheets and flash frozen so that future students of literature might be able to study under more realistic conditions what Patten calls "the state of the battered and bartered and lovely human soul."

I instructed the dealer to fax my final offer. It was just what the librarians had been waiting for.

A WRITER OF NEGOTIABLE VIRTUE

✻ "There is no such thing as inner peace," said Fran Lebowitz. "There is only nervousness and death."

For many writers there is only nervousness and deadlines. Karl Marx was already eighteen months late with *Das Kapital* when he received a letter from his publisher, saying that if they did not receive his manuscript immediately, they would be obliged to commission another author to do the work.

Fortunately my editor is more understanding. When I phoned to complain that I was suffering from columnist's burnout, that it was immoral, the amount of money I was earning, and how I was finding it harder and harder each week to make my deadline, she said, "Quit, why don't you? Do something different."

Starving would be different, but then what? With a lifetime of writing behind me I'm unqualified to do anything else. Besides, as Thoreau warns, "Distrust any enterprise that requires new clothes," which is another reason I've never changed careers. Writers don't need to dress respectably.

My husband's advice is to do what I love best. Now that writing has lost its appeal, that leaves reading, and sex. Bearing in mind those enterprising housewives you often read about in the court parade who, in order to make a little extra pocket money (in one case $6,000 a week), become hookers out of their own homes, I consider renovating my office.

A writer, after all, must be open to new experiences; as Ben Jonson said, "Who casts a living line, must sweat." My desk, on which piles of manuscripts lie waiting to be assessed, could be converted into a massage table; I'd find a circular bed to replace my vertical filing cabinet. I'd be able to hide my calendar, with deadlines circled in black, behind a smoked-glass mirror and screw a red light bulb into the swivel lamp attached to one of my bookcases.

The bookcases themselves, I got to thinking, might spoil the ambience. But a quick trip to the library to check out *The Madam as Entrepreneur: Career Management in House Prostitution* provided the solution.

While there may be a great number of figurative literary brothels, I read, the only actual *library* brothel in existence is in a St. Louis, Missouri, massage parlour. In the reading room a customer pays $20 for twenty minutes with a nude hostess who does nothing but read erotic literature to him.

I had my hook. My bookshelves could stay, and most of my books also. I certainly wouldn't have to go clothes shopping, and — I was already a good reader — wouldn't need to acquire any new skills. By working at home I'd be able to avoid some of the pits my sisters on the street corners fall into. One "lady of negotiable virtue" was actually prosecuted for biting a customer. "I was new to the job at the time," she said, "and I wasn't very good at it yet."

The concept of a library brothel might soften the blow, too, when my husband found out I was supplementing the family income with truly immoral earnings. It seemed a solution to all our problems — until I read further. "The customer may supply his own reading material if he desires, even things he has written himself."

There was the hitch. One reason I was having trouble making my deadlines was that ever since I'd agreed to read submissions to publishers (one major Toronto house receives upward of five hundred unsolicited manuscripts a week) and to write appraisals, I'd been inundated with other people's material.

It's one thing, though, to advise a hopeful writer, anonymously, not to give up the practice of law. But to sit nude across from him, reading his own erotic renderings ("His wiry body oozed with goose-bumpy joy. Sex is like swallowing a shard of glass — the pain moves through you constantly, a reminder that you are not empty.") for a loonie minute, I'd have to be crazy. I'm not *that* tired of column writing.

Still, $6,000 a week would come in handy, and I haven't completely scrapped the idea of moving in that bed. Then, if my editor called back wondering where next week's column was, I'd be in a suitable position to use one of Dorothy Parker's bon mots. Parker was also in bed when her editor at *The New Yorker* called, pressuring her for belated copy.

"Too fucking busy," Parker replied, "and vice versa."

TORTURING OUR WRITERS

❋ "In Argentina," says the bartender in a Robert Priest poem, "they torture their writers. In Canada they throw literary parties."

The best thing about literary parties is being invited to them. They can be deadly affairs. The American novelist Sherwood Anderson died of peritonitis after swallowing a toothpick with his hors d'oeuvre at a literary reception. Robert Greene, the sixteenth-century dramatist and pamphleteer, expired after a surfeit of complimentary wine at a banquet for authors. Even free drinks come with a price tag.

If they don't kill you, most literary parties leave scars. First there's the receiving line. While you wait to be introduced you try to think of something original to say to the queen of England.

Ahead of you in the lineup you recognize bill bissett. "You look raging in yellow," you hear him say to Her Majesty. "You're much more beautiful in person than on your stamps."

"And what do you do?" she inquires of bill, undaunted. He tells her he writes poetry. "What *sort* of poetry?" she asks, and bill presents her with his *end uv th world speshul,* chanting, "don't yu think we shud cum bfor yu go."

You no longer need to think of anything original. An orchestra plays "O Canada" as you shake hands all the way to the bottom of the receiving line where the media is waiting. They want to know why you aren't among the guests invited to the banquet after the reception. You're not about to tell them how, at your last royal dinner, you distinguished yourself by eating salad with your hands.

Most of the journalists, bureaucrats, artists, musicians, and cream of the literary establishment are already propping up the bar. All are trying to sort out who *isn't* here tonight. All are trying to figure out what their presence at this authors' reception says about their own reputations.

Then comes the first in a number of awkward moments. Before you've downed your first zombie, you find yourself clinking glasses, having to say, "Cheers, I like your work," to someone whose latest book you have just referred to as "evidence of a diseased mind" in a review, you hope, she hasn't read yet. Or, worse, you get cornered by the male critic whose use of derogatory adjectives in his attack on your haircut made you cancel all public appearances for the past month. He's chewing a cheap cheroot, which reminds you of T. S. Eliot's fondness for handing out exploding cigars to particularly egregious critics he met at literary receptions.

You don't air an opinion, but find another corner. Because you are a writer, strangers assume you wish to talk about yourself. So, before they ask what *you* do, you ask them what *they* do. Invariably you pick on world-famous personalities, such as the Duke of Edinburgh.

"We've met before, haven't we?" asks His Royal Highness when you've cleared up the matter of his identity. You wonder if he remembers you because you ate salad with your hands or because your new haircut was recently featured in a "makeover" article in a national magazine.

"What was your book called again?" he chats informally,

glancing at his watch. He wanders away before you have a chance to drop a royal brick and tell him you've written a dozen.

After some soggy canapés and more zombies, you are well on the way to airing your opinions. The worst situations are where you find yourself airing these to experts masquerading as fellow revellers. You ask Yehudi Menuhin if he's interested in music. You lecture the editor of the *Globe and Mail* on right-wing trends in journalism, and when you find out who he is, you say you didn't recognize him without his moustache, which he says he never had. You tell the head of the Canada Council there isn't enough money for writers because the bureaucrats spend it gallivanting about the country getting drunk on free drinks at literary receptions like this one. If the hors d'oeuvres don't kill you, somebody's look will.

So far tonight, though, you've been lucky. A guest at a literary party once asked Margaret Drabble whether she liked Margaret Drabble's "volumes of rubbish." Drabble says there are no answers to these kinds of questions. It is safer, she says, to give up social life altogether.

When the free drinks run out, dinner is announced. All guests except the authors head toward the banquet room, and bill bissett suggests we continue our party somewhere more festive. We settle on the El Mocambo.

As we're leaving, bill invites Her Majesty to join us. "You're probably a brilliant dancer," he tells her as the orchestra strikes up "God Save the Queen."

WRITING IT ALL OFF

※ "I love being a writer," says Peter De Vries. "What I can't stand is the paperwork." April brings an even crueller form of paperwork — the income tax return.

Every year I have to recalculate how much of my life is a

write-off. I remeasure the square footage of my whole house and divide it by my office space to determine maximum deductibility. I reestimate what my reasonable expectation of profit will be over the next three years, given my daily losses. But when it comes to reconciling my gross habits with my net income, I'm at a loss.

My husband suggests I call an accountant, but I don't need anyone else telling me how much of my life is a write-off. I retreat to my office with a fistful of T slips, Revenue Canada's *Instalment Guide for Individuals,* and an *Interpretation Bulletin.*

Any writer — even those who work for the government — should be possessed of the ability to write complete sentences in straightforward English. Halfway down the first sentence of the *Interpretation Bulletin,* I recall W. P. Kinsella's advice to writers: if you can't express yourself clearly, he says, abandon hope unless you are prepared to take a remedial English course.

I abandon the bulletin and open to page eight of the *Instalment Guide.* The bureaucratese here makes the bulletin look as simple as "See Spot run."

Take the sentence for taxpayers who are late. "The penalty is 50 percent of the amount, if any, by which the net instalment interest for the year exceeds the greater of a) $1,000 and b) 25 percent of the instalment interest calculated as if no instalment payment had been made for the year." In the time it takes to muddle through *that* bafflegab, *any* taxpayer would be late. The *Instalment Guide* lands beside the *Interpretation Bulletin* in the non-recyclable garbage.

I move on to the main event — the tax return itself. "STEP I — Usual First Name and Initial" is straightforward enough, providing I keep in mind one tax columnist's advice: "The worst thing a taxpayer can do is search between the lines of a tax form for deeper meaning. Just follow the instructions and do it line by line."

So far, so clear, until I get to Line 122: "Partnership income: limited or non-active partners only." This gets me thinking how

Susan Musgrave

non-active my husband has been since I've started bringing tax strategy booklets to bed . . . but then I think, just a minute here! What business has the tax department in the bedrooms of the nation?

I decide to tackle instead the less personal "personalized T7B-RF remittance form." By this point a simplified tax form suggested by Stanton Delaplane is starting to look good: "How much money did you make last year? Mail it in."

I am about to mail in my request for a personal interpreter, admit defeat, or apply for a government job where deductions are made at source. But then, as Graham Greene says: "We need not worry much about writers. Man will always find a means to gratify a passion. He will write, as he commits adultery, in spite of taxation."

The same goes for Woman. I file my return — in the junk mail drawer — and get back to a long poem about immortality. If I can find an ending, I'll sell it to the CBC. To offset my business expenses I need income.

Samuel Taylor Coleridge, in the middle of writing "Kubla Khan," was interrupted by a tax collector from Porlock. When the telephone rings, my "Person from Porlock" turns out to be a tax accountant from Price Waterhouse. He's read my columns and figures I need help. He suggests, to begin with, I take an inventory of my office supplies. I label my poem "To be continued . . ." and spend the rest of the day calculating how many staples I used for business during the 1989 tax year, and how many were for personal use.

Jules Renard once said that writing is the only profession in which one can make no money without looking ridiculous. During all the years I've spent not looking ridiculous, I've learned how to be creative. ("Income tax returns are the most imaginative fiction being written today," says Herman Wouk.) Inevitably my accountant phones to query the $19,345.23 I claim to have forked out for standard wire staples.

"Even so," he protests, "you claim you *spent* more than you *earned!*"

Doesn't everyone? Can't I write it off to experience?

THE LAPS OF CHARACTERS

❁ I had never suffered from writer's block. Surprise endings had always fallen into my lap. But my new story had reached its climax in a gazebo: my characters had run out of conversation and I didn't know what to do with them.

I went to the kitchen to make coffee instead. Just as I was putting the kettle on to boil, I overheard my daughter and her best friend discussing the facts of life. "Adultery is when you see your mother in the kitchen with another man," my daughter's friend explained.

It was the situation I'd been looking for. I shifted my characters from the gazebo into the kitchen, where the woman put the kettle on to boil. The man glanced at her wedding ring and . . . I began to yawn and shuffle my papers. Adultery wasn't easy; after three hours, I stopped trying and dragged my daughter to see *Honey, I Shrunk the Kids.*

The next day it was the same, and the day after that. Every time my characters attempted adultery they got stuck.

At first I refused to recognize my disease. I found myself staying in bed dreaming until lunchtime. I'm a morning writer, so with the morning gone I could proceed directly to the nonwriting portion of my day. If I went into my office at all, it would be to sort my paper clips, rearrange my bookshelves, or leaf through back issues of literary magazines.

It was in one of these that I tripped across a column on writer's block. "Exactly what is 'writer's block?'" asks Roger Caras, a writer and naturalist. "To quote Tevia in *Fiddler on the Roof,* 'Well, I'll tell ya, I don't know.'"

Susan Musgrave

I was about to toss the magazine when the word *symptoms* caught my eye.

"If you start to put the smaller size paper clips on one part of the clip holder on your desk and the larger size in another, you are showing signs of the early stages of the disease known as writer's block," Caras wrote.

My office had never looked so respectable. My wastepaper basket didn't even have a single piece of junk mail in it. Not only had I taken to reading my junk mail lately, I was even answering it.

When I got to the end of the article, I knew I was a sick writer. I had every one of the symptoms. I had the dreaded "block."

"Think positively about your craft," Caras suggested in his tips to recovery. "Consider the readers who are out there waiting for you to finish. Think of how pleased and proud of you your editor will be." If this aggravates the condition, he says, do something else creative besides write. Dance, whittle, garden, sketch — and if that doesn't work, try jogging. "There is nothing like worrying about chest pains to get you back in front of your desk."

I tried all the above, but every time I returned to my story my characters were still vertical in the kitchen.

In desperation I turned to other writers for solutions. "The best way for dealing with writer's block is never to get it," wrote John Gardner. "When I get writer's block, I walk around it," one writer told me, trying to be inspiring. Some were just discouraging: "When I hear about writer's block . . . Fuck off!" says Gore Vidal. "Stop writing for Christ's sake. Plenty more where you came from."

Help came in an article called "How to Get Unstuck" by Kelly Cherry, an American novelist. When she finds a man and a woman alone in a kitchen, she says, and she can't motivate them, at that point she always notices the coffee water on the stove is boiling over, the lid of the pot about to blow.

Musgrave Landing

"The woman reaches for the coffeepot; the steamed-up handle badly burns her hand, and, as she bravely pours the water into the cup in front of the man, her hand trembles, and hot water spills on the man's lap. He is horrified. The woman grabs a towel, runs it under cold water, kneels on the floor before him, and begins to wipe his lap dry."

The story, the author says, can go anywhere. "It has fallen into the character's lap, and, to speak no less plainly than Shakespeare, it is the laps of characters that hold the reader's attention."

It's a breakthrough! My story can go anywhere. But I also realize I've been preoccupied with adultery for so long I've been neglecting my own husband. I rush into the house to explain things.

I find my husband in the kitchen trying to boil water. The lid of the coffeepot is about to blow and, trying to be helpful, I reach for it.

BURIED IN A GRANT'S TOMB

❊ "It's a sad fact about our culture," W. H. Auden said, "that a poet can earn much more money writing or talking about his art than he can by practising it." Between writing about my art in the paper every other week, reviewing, judging contests, giving talks, conducting workshops, interviewing poets for magazines, composing articles on poetic technique, and reading *Mother Goose* to my kids, I had no time anymore to write my own poetry.

A grant was going to change all that. First I'd find a babysitter and then I'd change the world. . . .

Imagine my confusion when I was awarded the grant — $30,000, plus $2,000 for pencils and materials. On that amount I could live forever!

Susan Musgrave

I set to work at once, sending back *Incidents of Wife Battering in Contemporary Poetry: A Systems Theory Approach* to the poetry magazine I'd been reviewing for, telling them I'd be taking the rest of my life off. I cancelled classes, postponed readings, declined interviews. A week later, with nothing but a blank sheet in front of me, I sat down to write a poem.

Entitled "Poem Without Hope," it was the shortest poem I'd ever written, and I couldn't find an ending. In the months that followed I made more false starts.

Living, though, got easier. Nothing wrong with a bit of comfort, I convinced myself — even Saint Teresa could pray better when she wasn't wearing her hair shirt. But my problem was, I'd grown accustomed to poverty. It was hard to write poetry with security staring me in the face.

It didn't help when I came across William Faulkner's position. Writers don't need economic freedom, he said. All a writer needs is a pencil and some paper. "I've never known anything good in writing to come from having accepted any free gift of money. Good writers never apply for grants. They are too busy writing. If they're not first rate they fool themselves by saying they haven't got time or economic freedom."

But *I* had a grant and now I was stuck with it. Having accepted the money, I found, there was no procedure in which I could apply to give it back.

It wasn't that I was ungrateful to the Canada Council. But if gratitude, as La Rochefoucauld wrote, is merely the secret hope of further favours, I wasn't grateful, either. The grant had allowed me to live comfortably for a while, but it had also given me a whole new set of worries. What was I going to do when the grant ran out?

"Hundreds of writers have exhausted their grants and gone on to live happy productive lives," my husband tried to assure me.

"Like who?"

He named two. Both, I reminded him, had committed suicide.

And if I didn't write something soon, I was going to die also. My brain was already buried in a grant's tomb.

I decided to seek advice from writers who had never received grants. The government had invested in me $30,000 plus $2,000 for pencils — surely they deserved their money's worth? Some felt that if the state supports its artists, we need not feel indebted at all. Others disdained grants and spoke out against "feeding at the public trough." One poet reminded me of the professor who got a $10,000 grant to study prostitution in Winnipeg; she'd met him on the street where she was working to support *her* poetry habit.

A few romantics were skeptical about the utility of encouraging art of any kind on a grand scale. "Is encouragement what a poet needs?" asked one — a lawyer turned crime writer. "Open question. Maybe he needs *dis*couragement."

One month before my grant ran out I became discouraged enough about the future to start writing poetry. With my bank account now trying to hide under a duck, the pressure was again on. My entire writing life, from my first rejection slip to my most recent royalty cheque of $7.36, flashed before my eyes as I sat down to face my unfinished "Poem Without Hope."

By the time my final report was due to the Canada Council, my poem had reached epic proportions. I'd lived up to my end of the bargain — that is, I had produced — and lived well all the while.

"What is black and knocking at the door?" I posed in the final verse of my poem. "The future" was the hopeful note I ended on.

Susan Musgrave

PART II

Welcome, Suzanne Musrave

BOOT CAMP WITHOUT THE FOOD

✻ "Don't think you are superior to the people interviewing you on your book tour, especially the television people," Rita Mae Brown says in her feisty writer's manual, *Starting from Scratch*. No point in getting cranky just because they haven't had time to read your book. It's show business, and every third person wants to be on their television show. On her last book tour, for example, Brown sat in the greenroom next to a man who freeze-dried dead pets for a living.

In the greenroom I sit next to identical twins. They are sharing a muffin, which reminds me I haven't eaten since I arrived in Toronto the previous evening. It may be days before my next square meal. "A book tour is like boot camp without the food," I recall Brown saying as I have a quick fix of the freeze-dried cashews I've brought with me.

My publicist is in the midst of explaining that I've been invited to appear on national television because of my shock value as a writer, when the twins pop up on the greenroom monitor. They are both engaged, they reveal, to Death Row inmates who are scheduled for execution on the same day. As the twins chatter on about their plans to marry the men of their dreams in a double-ring ceremony before the double-noose ceremony takes place, I feel my shock value as a writer greatly decreasing.

Musgrave Landing

When it's my turn to face the nation at 8:00 a.m., I look to my publicist for some eleventh-hour advice. "You're a professional," she says. "Break a leg!"

But I needn't have worried. My host is a professional, too. He uses up most of my airtime telling his audience how my book is a classic, a Bible almost, a bestseller before it's even hit the stands. A telephone number flashes across the screen so that viewers can order their copies now while quantities last. Being a professional, I try to hide my dismay when he mispronounces both my name, *and* the name of my book.

En route to the next interview I assure my publicist I'm more talkative on radio. And, if the talk show host gets my name wrong, the whole of Canada can't see the hurt look on my face.

My publicist drops me in front of CLAM, where I am scheduled to be interviewed on this AM radio station's Oldies but Goldies hour. They don't usually have authors, my publicist has forewarned me, but are trying to become "culturally literate."

I take an elevator to the basement and wait there. When the fresh-faced disc jockey arrives, he is too late to "rap with me" (his words for pre-interview) but just in time to play the "oldie" that introduces me. Leonard Cohen sets the mood of the interview, singing "Suzanne takes you down." But halfway through the song the music dies and the disc jockey's voice rips the studio apart with, "That's Suzanne baby sockin' it to your perfect bod with her mind on rock till you drop. Today we have a living book writer. Welcome, Suzanne Musrave. You've written a book I'm sure going to read, and I want all you sex-crazed animals out there to read this book, too. Come on now, it won't hurt a bit, will it, Sue? More music coming right at you, so keep on rockin'!" I usher myself to the elevator. It's over that quick.

Back on the street, I flag down my publicist, who's had lunch. On the way to our next appointment I munch on some more nuts and, pulling up in front of the newspaper offices, knock back two miniatures of vodka left over from my flight. Brown says if you're going to get blasted, it will be in print. Blasted or not, this time I intend to *say* something.

"So . . . what makes you think you can write?" asks the ferret-faced sports reporter who's been assigned to cover books this week.

"Because my husband, who is two hundred pounds and knows how to use a chain saw, says I can." That's all he writes.

At dinnertime, down to my last handful of nuts, I arrive at an autographing session. Outside the bookstore I'm accosted by a man carrying a battered copy of my first book of poems on permanent loan from his local library. He has removed the dust jacket and wants me to write something "personal" under my bloodstained photograph.

I try to think of a safe dedication, remembering Rita Mae Brown's warning: "If you become the kind of writer who calls forth heated emotional states, be careful. There are a lot of unbalanced people out there. The statistics on insanity are that one out of every four people is suffering from some form of mental illness. Think of your three best friends. If they're okay, then it's got to be you."

Beneath my photograph I write: "It's got to be me."

GREAT EXPECTATIONS

❋ I'm watching *I Love Lucy* when the lady from the pottery shop phones. Someone has stopped to ask directions to my house. A poetry fan, she says — he has copies of my books he'd like me to sign. He's come all the way from Toronto. By bicycle.

I know the type. My fans nearly always ride bicycles. He'll have a ponytail and high ideals. My fans never arrive in limousines to take me to the Deep Cove Chalet for elegant meals. He won't have had a decent bite since he raided the dumpster behind Safeway on his way through Chilliwack two days ago. "Tell him where I live," I say resignedly.

The nerve, I think. Don't people realize that writers have to *work*? I switch off the TV and put on a scratchy recording of Dylan Thomas reading *Under Milk Wood* — probably what he expects to catch me listening to at this hour — then head into the bathroom.

I have exactly three minutes, the time it takes to pedal from the pottery shop, to transform. It's a big effort, having an image to live up to. I've been described as a tormented sea witch with "Medusa-like hair" who explores sexuality at the primal level of bone hurt; I hate disappointing people. I scrub the Clay and Ginseng Texturizing Mask off my face and borrow my husband's deodorant.

Within me is supposed to beat, according to the Montreal *Gazette*, a heart that welcomes flooding darkness in which to brew special magic. I don't feel like welcoming anything this morning — I stayed up last night making Rice Krispies squares — but my fan has arrived and is padlocking his bicycle, which isn't necessary on this part of the peninsula. He's obviously the insecure type who'll need more than just "Best Wishes" scribbled in my books. I slip out of my husband's pajamas and sift through the laundry basket for some passable clothes.

Dylan Thomas is rhapsodizing in Dolby; I choose the kind of book that only a poet who "writes of the possibilities inherent in human relationships, and the shadowy forces that can so easily destroy them," would read for pleasure — *The Executioner's Song* — and have it open at the page where Gary Gilmore says, "Let's do it," as my fan knocks. He is wearing a little sticker that says BE NICE TO ME I GAVE BLOOD TODAY and he looks as if he's going to faint when he reads *my* T-shirt, which says I EAT 'EM RAW, a gift from the opening of a friend's oyster bar. Hurriedly I throw a fringed shawl over my shoulders while my fan apologizes. He is sorry for arriving so unexpectedly, but he was "in the area, anyway."

"It's no problem," I say. He is fairly handsome, and I am forgiving by nature.

He takes off his rucksack, which is full of my slim, out-of-print volumes. My poetry, he says, is what has helped him cope ever since his girlfriend aborted their love child and married his best friend two months ago in Orillia. "My mother used to read your poetry, too," he adds. "In fact, she was reading one of your books the night she took the overdose."

"Please," I say to him, "come in."

I can see I'm not going to have to make any effort at all. I make tea instead while he empties his rucksack on the table. He asks me to inscribe *Grave-Dirt* to his youngest brother: "For Billy. I hope you recover." I'm supposed to have "extraordinary perceptual powers," so I dare not ask from what.

In another of my books he keeps a clipping from a Toronto newspaper where I am called the "enfant terrible of Canadian letters." I tell him when I hit forty they'll have to start dropping the enfant part, but he looks at me and doesn't laugh.

"I wrote a poem for you after I read that article," he said. "Would you like me to perform it for you? It's called 'Death of a Poet.'"

He's followed me into the kitchen, and he's breathing unevenly. I'd asked my husband to stay near the house and chop some wood so he would have the splitting axe handy if my fan turned out to be one of those psychotic persons. My husband, however, thinks I am indestructible. He has abandoned me and gone to the beach.

Death of a poet. I've never been less thrilled by the idea of performance poetry. I survey my weaponry — one rusty SOS pad and an aerosol can of Mr. Muscle oven cleaner. I don't want to die and give some critic the chance to say, "She asked for it, in her poetry."

But my fan turns out to have asthma, and the dagger I imagined is a poem, after all, nothing deadly. He reads, his voice quavering: a young poet sees how futile life is, and takes his own life on a mountain peak near Orillia. As far as I know, there aren't any peaks near Orillia, but the poem is so sincere that I become genuinely concerned about the young man's future and invite him to stay for lunch. It's the least I can do for one who has journeyed so far, and by bicycle.

"You're nothing like I expected you to be," he says, studying my face as I give him strong tea and a generous serving of Rice Krispies squares. No doubt he thinks those dark circles under my eyes are from staying up all night wrestling demons.

"Oh? What did you expect me to be like?" I ask, running my fingers through my Medusa-like hair.

"Like most people I've met," he says. "Sort of ordinary."

NONE RETURN FROM DEATH ROW

"Where can I find your book?" is a question authors are frequently asked. These days I hesitate before suggesting a bookstore.

The average trade book has a shelf life between that of milk and yogurt, says the author Calvin Trillin. With upward of fifty thousand books being published each year in the English language, it hardly surprises me when people ask the next question, "Why isn't your book in the bookstores?"

Lack of shelf space isn't the only reason. Of the fifty thousand published titles, any publisher's sales rep has a hundred new books to flog each season. This means the rep has roughly thirty seconds to interest a bookstore owner in your revised translation of the New Testament from Coptic into Latin. The buyer makes a snap decision, and before you know it, you have your grandmother on the line saying, "I looked all over town for your new book, but I couldn't find it in any of the libraries."

The publisher's sales rep has an answer for everyone. If your book isn't in the library, it's been checked out or stolen; if it's not in a bookshop, it means the book is selling. When your best friend complains that her corner store can't get hold of any copies, the sales rep says the store is on "credit hold" and will not be shipped any more books until the publisher is paid. And when your mother phones, thrilled that your book has sold every last copy she personally rearranged in front of Danielle Steele at Shopper's Drug Mart six weeks ago, the rep doesn't want to prick anybody's bubble but tells you, anyway, that the Drug Mart returned every last copy of your book to the publisher for credit.

Simon and Schuster started the book-return business. When they began allowing bookstores to return unsold copies, booksellers rewarded the publisher by prominently displaying their books in windows, or next to the cash register under a sign marked BESTSELLER. Other publishers were forced to make the same arrangements. "Gone today, here tomorrow," said Alfred Knopf as the returns poured into his storerooms.

Today about half the books shipped to wholesalers get returned. While most hardcover books are shipped back intact, a great many unsold paperbacks go to the shredder after the covers have been ripped off and submitted for credit.

How can a writer prevent her book from being sent back to nourish the larvae of silverfishes and book lice in some publisher's warehouse? One thing she can do is sign every book in sight. Bookstores can't return books that have been written in by their authors.

When my new book was published, just in time for Christmas, I went to autograph copies at one of Vancouver's biggest bookstores. But there were no copies in sight! The manager tracked them down in her computer and told me to wait while she went downstairs to "dig them up" out of the Essays section. She reached under the counter for a flashlight.

I'd spent hours in the lonely Poetry corner of this bookstore; I could direct anyone who was really lost to the shelves of Canadiana. But in all the book-buying years of my life I'd never encountered an Essay section.

It was more of a *row* than a section, the manager confessed, when she emerged with books for me to autograph. "Death Row" was what her employees jokingly called it — on a good day.

I signed both my volumes and clutched them to my breast, as I did when I found copies of my only novel in Smithbooks under a HURT BOOKS sign. "Your essays are in good company — right next to Montaigne's," the manager added defensively. I'd rather be in Alan Fotheringham's company *any* day. *His* essays formed a pyramid in the bookstore's front window.

But there was one consolation. As long as my book remained on Death Row, there would be no returns. Montaigne's *Essays* had probably slept there since they were published in 1588. No one working in the bookstore would be able to *find* our books in order to rip the covers off and send the contents to be pulped.

"The only thing more difficult than being a writer is being a happily published one," say the editors of *The Writer's Home Companion.* "For once the book is written, the baby is born. The gestation period might have taken months or years but it is then put in the hands of someone else to care for it."

Woebetide the book that falls into the hands of a bookseller.

SHE WHO LAUGHS, LASTS

❋ Winning, I tell myself as I sip the stars out of a glass of champagne, is not a matter of life or death. It's more important than that.

Susan Musgrave

At least my publisher must think so. This is the first time the firm has booked me in Executive Class — I've been short-listed for the Stephen Leacock Medal for Humour and the J. P. Wiser Cash Award. Even the flight attendant, when he catches me laughing aloud at my own book, bumps me up to First Class. Not, as it turns out, because he thinks I'm *somebody*, but so I won't disturb other passengers. The First Class cabin is empty.

"It would be tempting fate to have written my acceptance speech before the winner was announced, so I haven't prepared one," I write, preparing my acceptance speech — just in case. Realistically, what were the chances of winning?

Andreas Schroeder says if we have a beauty contest in Canada, we give the prize to the runner-up, because the one who deserves to win already has enough going for her. I figured I had as much chance as the next man — I was the only woman short-listed. But even if I won, I doubted I'd be able to answer the skill-testing question.

"Everything becomes symbol and irony when you have been betrayed," Jay McInerney wrote in *Bright Lights, Big City.* Everything becomes symbol and irony when you are awaiting the announcement of a "more important than life or death" award. For instance, when my editor meets my plane and whisks me into the bright lights of Toronto for a previctory dinner, I don't have to dig far to find the deeper meaning in my fortune cookie: "Victory is iffy."

"What is important? Jokes and luck." These are the next fortuitous words I open to in Alice Munro's *Friend of my Youth* the next morning while waiting for my publicist to drive me to the hospital grounds. That the award winner is being announced in a place for sick people, speaks volumes about Canadian humour.

It didn't bode well from the minute I pinned my name tag through my left breast. To add insult, my name had been spelled incorrectly. When my publicist introduced me to the chairperson of the awards committee, who insisted on being called the chair*man*, she looked my patched jeans over and asked, "Where does *she* come from?"

"She's from British Columbia. I think she's one of our finalists," prompted another committee member.

But what serious writer of humour would be discouraged by the fact that the Awards Committee hasn't read her book? Instead I did what Leacock's Lord Ronald did: said nothing, and flung myself madly from the room in all directions. As luck would have it, I landed at the bar alongside a talk show host who remembered interviewing me years ago, "after you won one of your first awards." I didn't want to disillusion him by saying the only thing I'd ever won was a Frequent Flyer Award from Air Canada. I earned it by accumulating mileage points flying to receptions for prizes I'd been nominated for.

"Anybody who has listened to certain kinds of music, or read certain kinds of poetry . . . will admit that even suicide has its brighter aspects," Stephen Leacock once said. Anybody who has suffered through certain kinds of luncheons will admit the same.

The press is out in force, but of the writers short-listed, only three others have materialized. The chairman introduces us after we've cleaned our plates of crôissants stuffed with fresh B.C. crab. I'm last on the list. "She's come all the way from British Columbia, *just for lunch!*"

The crab and I. Well, victory had been iffy, anyway. "I'd been hoping it wasn't *just* for lunch," I replied. Jokes and luck. At least I got the laughs.

After I posed with the three other contenders ("Isn't this wonderful?" cried an observer. "All the *losers* being photographed . . ."), my publicist dropped me at Eve Et Lui's in Yorkville where I spent the equivalent of the J. P. Wiser Cash Award on stretch jeans with designer patches.

My friend Arlene, who drove me to the airport because I had no money left for cab fare, was convinced I didn't win because I hadn't become respectable enough. A little respect is a good thing for a writer, I concluded as I ran for my flight, price tag fluttering from my new jeans — but I'd never want to become *too* respectable.

ANOTHER PERFORMER FOR LITERACY

�֍ These days when a book of stamps costs more than a book of poetry, Canada Post had nerve inviting me, a poet, to speak at their convention. A "new policy would be unveiled to stamp out literacy" is what I *thought* the spokesperson said.

Before I could say they had gone *too* far this time, she repeated her request. Canada Post wanted me to speak at the unveiling of a new *postage stamp* for literacy.

The spokesperson promised to send me an "information package." It arrived in the mail, eventually. At least there were no glossy, full-colour brochures like ones the government distributed last year: "ILLITERATE? If you can't read this, you need help. Send a self-addressed stamped envelope to . . ." Whoever wrote that must have taken Alberto Moravia's words at face value: "Nowadays the illiterates can read and write."

I scanned the program to find my place. Early in the day came the celebrities "rockin' and readin'" their way through a musical tribute to literacy. Before lunch the dignitaries would unveil the stamp (which meant speeches) and politicians would announce new literary programs (more speeches). Then, at the end of the day, after refreshments and a video presentation called *Flight for Freedom* (which the speeched-out audience would probably take advantage of, literally), came the writers. Why is it that authors, the people who write the books we're all encouraged to read, always come last? I plotted a speech on this subject, although I scrapped it when I recalled the coordinator saying there would be children present. The topic she'd suggested was: "Reading to Children Can Improve Literacy."

I wouldn't have time to write a long speech because my latest little despot expects me to read to her these days, on demand. She knows *Curious George* by heart, and at eighteen months can point out the mouse on every page of *Goodnight Moon*, even the one where the mouse lurks behind a bowlful of mush. I convince myself that it is all in the name of improving literacy, but by the time I get to my office every morning, my brain has become mush.

I just need to write enough of a speech to justify getting my travel costs reimbursed, but . . . is there anything left that *hasn't* already been written about literacy? In search of an idea I dip into a book called *When Writers First Learned to Read* and learn how many writers, as children, were discouraged from reading. William Butler Yeats, for instance, was given the choice between going to church or (a fate worse than church!) staying home and reading poetry. Rudyard Kipling's guardians forced him to read under fear of punishment. When it became clear that books provided him with an escape from unhappiness, deprivation from reading was added to his punishments.

There's a novel idea. I could deliver a speech saying maybe we're not doing our kids a favour by teaching them to read before they can walk. If we really want them to love books, should we lock *Curious George* under the sink with the household poisons?

By the time International Literacy Day arrives, I'm worn out from spending sleepless nights trying to come up with something to say. I catch the earliest ferry to Vancouver and arrive at Canada Place where the dignitaries and rock stars have come, scarfed their free lunches and, like half the audience, gone. I pin a badge saying Another Performer for Literacy to my breast and go to the greenroom in search of help.

"Tell jokes," suggests John Gray.

"Wing it," says Spider Robinson, who must have devoted most of International Literacy Year to typing his five-hundred-page dissertation. Still speechless, I'm creeping through the darkened auditorium toward the emergency exit when a person no bigger than a fire hydrant approaches me with a request.

John brings the house down with his one-liners, Spider's essay will be nominated for a Nobel, no question, but when I get on-stage and quote, from memory, "Once upon a time there was a little monkey. His name was Curious George, and he was very curious," the children give me a standing ovation.

Leaving the stage, I get a hug from the coordinator, and an envelope. I open it immediately, but there's nothing inside. The coordinator whispers that it's a gift from Canada Post — a collector's item first-day cover of the National Literacy stamp.

"But what about my travel expenses?" I shouldn't have asked. It's every writer's nightmare. The cheque's in the mail.

HERE TODAY GONE TO MAYO

✳ "Give me a drink. I only want to live," says the man at the table next to me, the only other customer in the bar. I'm touring the Yukon for the week-long National Book Festival, and killing time.

I keep my head in a book. "The true writer has a great advantage over most people," John Gardner writes. "He knows the great tradition of literature, and fits himself to the company he most respects and enjoys: the company of Homer, Vergil, Dante, and Shakespeare."

"You looking for company?" asks the man who, a moment ago, only wanted to live. I close *The Art of Fiction* as he gets up and lurches toward the washrooms, which are marked BOSSES and SECRETARIES. I don't stay to see which door he bumps into. I have an autographing session at Books on Main.

In the bookstore, which also sells souvenirs, I am given a stool at the counter. Behind me the sourdough starter is on sale, and it turns out to be the main attraction. By four o'clock I've sold it all, plus two pewter figurines on iron pyrite and a legendary Alaska Ulu knife from the glass case on top of which my overlooked volumes are stacked. When sales slack off, I read the entertainment ads in the *Yukon News.* I can enjoy an evening meal at Sam 'n Ella's up Main Street, and afterward catch a film called *Sammy and Rosie Get Laid* — "a knee-to-groin experience guaranteed to upset all advocates of good taste."

Next to this announcement I find my own name. I'll be reading from my work at public schools and prisons in the area, with the grand finale on Friday in a psychiatric institute.

By the end of the autographing session I've sold two books, both by Pierre Berton. The news agent says he'd like to see Stephen King in the Yukon for National Book Festival next year: "a passionate kind of guy." I return to my hotel with *The Art of Fiction* and spend the rest of the weekend boning up on the author-participant point of view.

Early Monday we're on the road. We have breakfast at a truck stop offering Rolaids on the menu, which doesn't bode well. Mary, my host, tells me that her Presbyterian upbringing forbids her to cut her toenails on a Sunday, and that every time her husband swears, she makes him pay a quarter to a society for lepers. This doesn't bode well, either.

"'Sanity in a writer involves taste,'" I tell the fifty-odd students poised on the edges of their seats in the Mayo school library. I have memorized most of Gardner's book on the five-hour drive up here. "'To write as Shakespeare wrote, so that people understand, sympathize, see the universality of pain and feel strengthened . . .'"

A teacher interrupts, wanting to know how I feel, given what I've just said, about my first novel, which deals with a young girl coming of age in a commune full of sex-crazed cannibals. I dodge the question by telling her I'd assumed my novel would have been banned in Yukon schools, as it had been in other parts of the country.

Susan Musgrave

A student interrupts, wanting to know where my novel is available and what pages the "good parts" are on. I dodge the subject by changing it. "Anyone name a Canadian author?" I ask.

"Robert Service," ventures one.

"Stephen King," says another with passion.

After my presentation, Mary and I have dinner with the school principal. The lodge he takes us to doesn't have Rolaids on the menu, although by the end of the meal I am looking for some. The principal has taught students in this remote community for six years and wears a T-shirt reflecting his worldview: HERE TODAY GONE TO MAYO. He gives me the impression that, for him, *book* is a four-letter word, and admits, over meat loaf, that he has never found a Canadian worth reading. When dessert comes, he asks, "What is the difference between Canada and yogurt?" I am reluctant to admit that I can't answer.

"Yogurt has a living culture," he says, pleased.

A true writer has a great advantage over most other people in that she can string together a list of expletives a mile long without repeating herself once. I wait until the principal has gone before expressing my true opinion of his views, then write Mary a $20 cheque — for the lepers. Mary, who has proven — next to Homer, Vergil, Dante, and Shakespeare — to be the best company I could have hoped for, tears the cheque in half. We spend the money on Harvey Wallbangers instead.

"Give me a drink. I only want to live through the National Book Festival": my new motto. By Friday I was ready for the psychiatric institute.

GREAT ONE GOES

❋ The poster says: "We have a prophetess in our midst. She will be reading her poetry August 9 at 8:00."

In Toronto in 1987 I read on Black Monday after the stock

market crash, in Sudbury after INCO laid off two thousand workers, and now I've arrived in Edmonton where the headlines scream GRETZKY TRADED. If I were a true prophetess, I wouldn't be reading again on the eve of another disaster.

The imposter, with six-year-old daughter in tow, climbs a flight of stairs to the Off-the-Wall Gallery. The walls are covered with etchings of mutilated organs; my daughter wants to know what they mean. I'm about to tell her that all art should be, not mean, when the artist introduces himself. I avert my eyes from his *Ovarian Cyst* while he explains how his vision complements my poetry.

Early in my career I felt duty-bound to read my most depressing stuff — poems of despair and tortured love, of failed suicide and unrequited lust. I had a dedicated following. In Winnipeg one winter, for instance, I read to a handful of homeless derelicts who had come to the library to get warm. They even applauded after every poem — to warm their hands. One, with newspapers wrapped around his feet in place of shoes, came up to thank me when the reading was over. My poetry, he said, had been an inspiration — to end it all that night.

At this point my perspective changed. I didn't want a successful poetry reading to be one where people felt like slitting their throats after listening to me, so I switched to stand-up comedy. I'm not sure that anyone noticed.

The Off-the-Wall Gallery is packed; it was built to seat fifty. I'm used to giving poetry readings in this kind of space. I'll be expected, afterward, to help stack the chairs.

The director of the gallery comes forward to introduce me. After being touted, once again, as a prophetess, I begin my reading.

In Canada, I tell my expectant audience, hockey is the poetry of the masses. To press my point, I ask how many hockey fans there are in the crowd. When no hands are raised, I tell them the reason for there being only fifty people here tonight is that the other fifty thousand have stayed home, mourning the loss of the Great One.

What if there should come a time, I prophesize, when poets, like hockey players, are treated as depreciating assets and traded by publishers for hard cash to foreign countries: "Canada lost its finest poet Tuesday," the papers might report, "when Margaret Atwood was dealt to Los Angeles in the most stunning poetry deal in history. She packed her word processor and the best years of her life and headed south . . . to what? To millions of Los Angelenos who don't give a damn, to a town that doesn't know a poetry book from a surfboard. . . ."

The expectant faces have become incensed. Once again I am being taken deadly seriously.

"In Toronto," I continue, undeterred, "before the deal was announced, outraged poetry fans jammed all incoming phones to her publisher. One NDP MP argued against free trade in poets. He urged the federal government to stop the sale of Margaret Atwood, saying she is a national symbol, like the beaver."

Having thoroughly convinced my audience, I launch into my first poem, "Two Minutes for Hooking." I wrote it ten years ago, but it seems downright prophetic now. "You are leaving," it begins. When I finish the poem, the room is so quiet you can hear hearts breaking.

We take our symbols seriously. After the reading, I am overwhelmed by fans. I autograph books, I shake hands. For fifteen minutes I'm famous, until I catch my daughter, who's always been my most reliable critic, looking skeptical in a corner.

I push through the crowd. "Well, how did I rate?" I ask when she isn't forthcoming.

"Did you see the size of my yawn, Mum?" she replies. Peter Pocklington says Gretzky has an ego the size of Manhattan; my ego shrinks to the size of the *Ovarian Cyst* on the wall of the Off-the-Wall Gallery.

When the audience has gone, my daughter shows me how to

put away the chairs. She makes it clear I'm a mother first of all. I may be a great one, but I'm still a depreciating asset.

DECLAIMING AGAINST THE WIND

✳ The American poet Louis Untermeyer once returned his lecture fee to a group of struggling poets and told them to put the money to good use. When later he inquired what good use they had chosen, he learned the group had started a fund to "get a better speaker next year."

Authors, through the ages, have rarely been brilliant public speakers. But these days, in an atmosphere of literary vaudeville and book-plugging mania, more and more writers are accepting speaking engagements. If there's a chance it will sell a book, most authors will speak to anyone.

So, naturally, without inquiring what The Conference of Emerging Voices is, I agree to be their after-dinner speaker. I don't dare ask, "Why me?" either. The last time I asked I was told a more important writer wasn't available.

My bus arrives, five hours late, in a northern Ontario blizzard. The cabbie who drives me to the community centre says he has no idea who my audience will be, or if, on a night like this, I'll even *have* one.

"If you want an audience in this town, start a fight," he says, leaving me in the handicapped zone.

I struggle in out of the storm with my suitcase of books. A sign pinned to the door says PROTESTANT BINGO CANCELLED TONIGHT. I stand thawing on the doormat until a man wearing his table napkin as a bib comes to greet me.

"You must be our poet!" he exclaims, identifying himself as chairperson of the Speaker's Committee. He doesn't offer to lug my heavy suitcase up the stairs as he tells me how much he appreciates me coming. It is crucial, he feels, for the sufferers of speech disorders to get a chance to hear brilliant speakers.

"Why me?" I'm on the verge of crying out as we reach the hall where my select audience is gathered around the bar. The chairperson points me to the head table where a fisherman-type is having a case of beer. Personally I'd like to eat something. I'd assumed there would be a dinner before my after-dinner speech.

"I'm afraid we had to start without you, but if you're hungry, I'm sure we can scrape up something," says the chairperson, removing his bib before turning to address the crowd.

"Fellow sufferers," he begins, once they are all seated. "It's time to introduce this evening's entertainment. Six months ago our friend — " he points to the fisherman-type next to me " — was like you. He couldn't speak a word. Now, thanks to all the wonderful people who made donations at our last year's conference, he not only talks, he sings!"

The fisherman rises to deafening applause and belts out, "If Today Was a Fish, I'd Throw It Back In." His voice — pure and melancholic — fills the hall. The audience is on the verge of tears. We give him a standing ovation.

The chairperson begins his "few words by way of an introduction" about me. Half an hour later he's reminding us he wasn't always able to speak at this length in front of an audience. At one time he was the victim of a stammer. Through sheer perseverance he overcame his impediment the way the great Greek orator Demosthenes did, by placing pebbles in his mouth and declaiming against the wind.

"Ladies and gentlemen, we have another great orator with us this evening. She came all the way from Vancouver Island to speak to you and recite her poetry." He pauses as a fish, which should have been thrown back in, is scraped up for me from the kitchen. By now my appetite has evaporated. I'm feeling inadequate. Tongue-tied.

Why me?

"All of you here would like to be great poets," the chairperson continues. "Poetry is what you aspire to. It is not by any amount of material splendour but only by moral greatness, by words, by works of imagination, that you, the voiceless, can have a voice in the future."

What, after that, can I possibly tell these people? I'm halfway to my feet when I get a reprieve; three disgruntled bingo players come in out of the cold, determined it will be bingo as usual. The chairperson asks them, politely, to leave, and they become vociferous. The fisherman tells them to step outside. My whole audience follows.

It takes time to fight it out; when the police arrive, it takes more time to sort it out. The survivors trickle back inside, but by this time it's too late for poetry. I show them my books instead. I intend, I tell everyone, to return my speaker's fee, *plus* any money from book sales, to help them in their struggle.

The chairperson carries my empty suitcase from the hall, assuring me they'll put my money to good use. "Next year," he says, "we'll be able to afford Margaret Atwood."

DECODING FOR THE AGENTS OF CHAOS

�֍ "'The purpose of education is not to know forever the functions of the cell membrane or the capital of Uruguay,'" I read from an article by Crawford Killan. "'It is to know how to learn fast in the face of chaos, which means built-in unpredictability.'"

I'm addressing two hundred English teachers at their annual spring conference. After "decoding the mythos of literature," I open the floor for questions. I've got time to kill before the bar reopens and normal life resumes.

"Given what you've just said about the purpose of education," says a teacher in a Grateful Dead T-shirt, "what about the role of the educator?"

Susan Musgrave

64

"Educators are agents of chaos," I say, cribbing from Killan again. "By making your students less predictable, you ensure their freedom."

It sounds lofty, and I'm resting on Killan's laurels when a soft-spoken teacher from Thunder Bay pulls the wreath out from under me. "I've got forty-five fifteen-year-olds who prefer smoking crack to studying postmodernism. I've never had to worry about any of them being predictable."

So much for lofty theories. Luckily the next questioner asks something I can answer from experience. "Is it essential for a writer to have a formal education?"

"Charles Dickens and Mark Twain didn't even finish grade school," I reply. "Jack London dropped out of high school and Emile Zola got 0 in French literature. Woody Allen says he was thrown out of college for cheating on the metaphysics exam; he looked into the soul of the boy sitting next to him."

"Perhaps you can tell us the reason *you* dropped out of high school?" asks the spitting image of my grade ten home economics teacher, who urged me to upgrade my baby-sitting skills.

"I looked into the soul of home ec," I tell her, "and saw no future."

She writes that down. All the teachers, I suddenly notice, are writing down every word I utter.

"Would you go so far as to blame the education system for the fact you became a writer?" asks one, who is also recording my answers on a pocket-size tape recorder.

I don't blame the system, I say. I am grateful to it. I explain how my creative juices started flowing when I began to forge notes from my parents with excuses why I couldn't participate in phys ed. I am thankful to my phys ed teacher for making me do time in the library after school. I spent hours in the stacks reading all kinds of modern poetry and discovered, among others, Irving Layton. I didn't know poetry was even *allowed* to have four-letter words in it. His early poetry changed my life.

"You say you enjoyed reading rude poems at school," the teacher who is taping me continues, "but don't you feel poetry should be used as a springboard to higher thinking?"

"Give kids poems they can identify with," I reply, "poetry that encourages lower thinking. No high school student wants to analyze the metaphors in Earle Birney's "David," or figure out what T. S. Eliot "really means." Read them that Charles Bukowski poem with the f-word in it instead. Chances are, everyone in your class will have heard the f-word before," I continue, decoding poetry for the agents of chaos, "and be fully aware of its connotations."

We're running out of time, and the teachers are scribbling faster. "Any kid who makes it as far as grade twelve knows what Joe Hall really means when he writes: 'I'm fucking jaded and I want more drugs,'" I assure them.

All are writing furiously — ". . . want . . . more . . . drugs." The teacher in the Grateful Dead T-shirt glances at his Rolex when he asks me, "What about you? Did *you* use drugs in high school?"

"Not *in* school," I reply, "but in the parking lot behind the school. Someone said if you remember the sixties, you weren't really there. Well, I don't remember the lunch hours."

I'm giving them plenty of time to get it all down, but the Dead fan keeps looking over his shoulder at the clock. "Many of us here are children of the sixties," he says finally, closing his notebook, "but what do you say now to *this* generation?"

"Tell them, if they really want to get high, read poetry. As a teacher, you can help by inviting living writers — Canadian writers — to come to your schools." William Wordsworth is pushing up daffodils, I tell my audience, but Al Purdy is available.

"You've done a whole lot of living," the Dead fan wraps up. "Have you ever considered teaching as a profession?"

I hear glasses clinking as the bar opens next door.

"Teaching has ruined more novelists than drink," I say, quoting Gore Vidal to the teachers. Some are still writing as I head for the bar.

WHERE AUTHORS FEAR TO TEACH

✳ I was fourteen when I dropped out of high school and ran away from home to pursue a literary career. After freezing all afternoon on the railway tracks near Ladysmith, writing lyrical poems about smokestacks and factories, I almost welcomed the police who came to drag me home again.

My father said, "Get your education and the world will be your oyster." I dropped back in to high school, where poetry became my favourite subject. I was good at finding hidden meanings but bad at counting metaphors and similes. Analyzing poetry seemed a way of avoiding the real issues. Before I turned fifteen I'd left school for good.

Twenty years later, although still not qualified to attend university, I became writer-in-residence at the University of Waterloo and taught advanced creative writing on the side. It was a two-year position, and I got hooked on that monthly paycheque. As my job drew to a close, I considered my options: unemployment and welfare. I was feeling so low that I even considered enrolling in university. I could get my education. Get a job teaching. Get tenure. The world would be my oyster.

The day I sat down to fill out an application, a parcel arrived, an anthology called *Inside Poetry*, meant to be used as a creative writing text. One of my poems was included.

Question: "Why do you think Musgrave divided this poem into four stanzas?"

I counted the stanzas and thought — it just happened that way. I'd divided the poem because it looked good on the page.

"Is this poem optimistic or pessimistic?" the editors posed. "Defend your answer with quotations from the poem."

A critic once pointed out that most of my positive love poems were written in transit. I'd always thought "Crossing to Brentwood on the Mill Bay Ferry" was one of those optimistic moments, but when I looked at it, and looked at it again, I wasn't so sure. When I realized I couldn't answer any of the questions about my own poem, I scratched the idea of getting a university education.

That fall I was hired to teach short fiction at a local community college. I was determined to be a conscientious teacher. Although I'd written short fiction all my life, I prepared for my classes by reading endless books that told me how to go about doing it. "Write about what you know," says Ernest Hemingway. "Writing about what you know will fill pages with dull and uninteresting material," says W. P. Kinsella. The more I learned, the less sure I became. "All knowledge is loss," says the poet R. E. Rashley.

A week before class started I phoned my students to ask them to bring a recent story and a sharp pencil to our first session. I got through to all eleven women on my list but couldn't reach the sole male who'd registered. I got his answering machine.

"Hello, this is God," came a voice. "I have no time to speak to mere mortals like you. . . ." He commanded me to leave a message after the beep, but by this time I'd forgotten why I'd even called.

The night of my first class, God didn't show. For half an hour I spoke to my students' concerns about love, eternity, war, and the meaning of life. Then came the hard questions, the ones I'd hoped they wouldn't ask. Can writers be made, or are they born that way?

I suggested we look for answers in their work. The first volunteer read a story, written in the first person, about a woman who didn't find housework creative. Her husband gets home late demanding "a goddamn beer" and "Where's dinner?" He fails to notice that the casserole, and his wife's head, are in the gas oven. I avoided the story's real problem by analyzing the point of view.

The same husband-wife dynamic occurred in many of the women's stories. The men were ugly and the women were sad. By the end of the evening I was wishing God had arrived. He might have provided some comic relief.

"You should hear what their husbands say to them," I told my own husband, who had my slippers and Ovaltine ready when I arrived home after the class. "I've never had men talk to *me* like that."

"You never listened," my husband said.

Next term the college wants me to teach poetry. I was leafing through *Inside Poetry* to see how it was done when I came across "Puff the Magic Dragon," the song made popular by Peter, Paul, and Mary in the sixties.

"What did Jackie Paper have to gain from his relationship with Puff?" the editors suggested I ask.

I made a note: "To be discussed." I was starting to get the hang of it.

SCABBING FOR CLARITY

❈ The CIA has an assassination unit called the Health Alteration Committee. I'm reading the paper. A banker describes his loss as a "net profits revenue deficiency."

Another article, headed CANADIANS ENTITLED TO A JUSTICE SYSTEM THEY CAN UNDERSTAND, states: "When a person gives you an orange, he simply says, 'Have an orange.' But a lawyer will say, 'I hereby give and convey to you, all and singular, my estate and interest, right, title, claim and advantage of and in said orange, together will all its rind, juice, pulp and pips and all rights and advantages therein with full power to bite, suck and otherwise to eat the same or give the same away with or without the rind, juice, pulp and pips, anything hereinbefore or hereinafter . . . etc.'" Surely we are entitled to at least one official language we can understand, also.

I'm preparing a lecture on the abuses of jargon (root sense: bird twitter, gibberish) for my creative writing class. "Don't write, 'Gloria was unable to reevaluate her role in the interconnectedness of all life because she was undergoing an ego integrative action hormonal displacement," I'd pleaded with one student. "Just say, 'Gloria was confused.'"

"Don't use *humongous*, say *huge*," I'm always begging.

It's usage abusage, but abusers can't be blamed. The way English composition is taught at school tends to foster wordiness and obscurity. Students learn to shirk responsibility for their feelings by using flowery adjectives and passive verbs, by making vague generalized statements. One, for instance, who plans to teach creative writing, wrote: "The power we ascribe to a poem is answered by another power, that of a reading adequate to it in principle and by intention, if inadequate to the event." Translation: You get out of it what you put into it.

And when I urge my students to write more clearly, they tell me they can't afford to. If they take my advice, they'll never get through law school, or a decent job in business. There would be no future in government or politics. They could never teach English at a major university.

Heard the one about the poststructuralist mafia? They make you an offer you can't understand. Academics are some of the worst offenders when it comes to making simple ideas sound complicated. For "complexity and obscurity have professional value," says John Kenneth Galbraith. "They are the academic equivalents of apprenticeship rules in the building trades. They exclude outsiders and keep down competition. The man who makes things clear is a scab. He is criticized less for his clarity than for his treachery."

I decide to make a hit list of jargoneers, starting with all lawyers and academics, when Frank, the computer expert, phones. My computer has been in the shop for a week, but as it turns out "the relocatable machine-code program is turned into an executable, absolute machine code by the linker, CLINK . . ."

"Does this mean the thingummijig will still be skewiff when I switch on the little whatchamacallit at the back?" I retaliate.

While I'm on hold I open the day's mail. A form letter from my tax accountant advises that, "in accordance with the GST, you are liable for your *actual* hypothetical tax." I'm adding accountants to my hit list when Frank comes back on the line, assuring me "the machine code also merges the user's program with previously compiled program files." Computer specialists go down on my list, also.

In today's mail, too, there's a copy of a new magazine called *Geist*, which contains an excerpt from a third-year English exam given recently at a major Canadian university. "Define each of the following terms and give examples from novels you might have read: a) anti-Gothic convention; b) mock-epic simile; c) unreliable narrator; d) the convergence of terms that are normally widely separated; e) generalized tmesis; g) chiasmus; h) nesting structure; i) collapse of language into a fearful synonym of principle of identity," reads the first question.

I'm hoping I never need to know what generalized tmesis is (are), and I'm still pondering the root sense of chiasmus when I hand out copies of the English exam to my class that evening. I offer an A+ to anyone who can tell me what this question *means*.

It's an offer they understand. "No jargon," I warn as I hold up my hit list, which I'm submitting to the Health Alteration Committee. "Whoever uses jargon is in for it."

PERISH AND BE READ?

❃ The professor had brought banned books to the classroom to tempt his English students into reading. When even that didn't work, he'd invited me — "a living author" — to appear for National Book Festival. During question period, he asked me to recommend some new "lively" novelists.

"'Roll over Dash Hammett and tell Jean Genet the news — Seth Morgan has qualified to *signify*,'" I quote, flashing the wild author photo on the book's back cover. "'Five'll get the reader ten — before he's set down *Homeboy*, his sides will be split, his heart broken . . . and his short hairs fried.'"

That ought to get their attention. This novel, in fact, did more than the blurb promised, and I ended up writing my first fan letter. Then, less than a year after *Homeboy* was published, Seth Morgan — ex-con, ex-addict, ex-lover of Janis Joplin (who died herself a few months before her only number one hit, "Me and Bobby McGee," was released) had been killed in a motorcycle accident.

"What was that name again?" asks a biker-type in studded leather, with RIP tattooed between his eyebrows. Thinking I've managed to hook one reader, I repeat Morgan's name. "It's not for me," the student blurts out before his classmates get the wrong impression. "I've got this friend who only reads dead authors."

There's an Italian proverb: "The best way to receive praise is to die." I rack my brain to come up with more dead lively authors, like John Kennedy Toole, whose only novel *The Confederacy of Dunces*, published in 1976, was posthumously awarded the Pulitzer Prize. Twelve years earlier, Toole, depressed because he couldn't find a publisher, had committed suicide.

And then there was my own close friend. Tom York had achieved some critical acclaim with his four novels and a "spiritual autobiography," *And Sleep in the Woods* (he was ordained a

United Church minister in 1967), but was on the verge of making his big breakthrough when he was killed in a car accident in 1988. *Desireless*, Tom's final novel, was published posthumously. For this book he received the highest praise.

Nowadays, thanks to posthumous publishing, even a writer with no pulse can have a literary career. Raymond Chandler, dead for thirty years, had a new release (*Poodle Springs*) recently; western writer Louis L'Amour died in 1988 but continues to be prolific — four posthumous books have been published to date. "While these new titles may not be their authors' most polished efforts," writes Gregory Cerio (*Newsweek*, February 5, 1990), "they are a boon to publishers and writers' heirs alike. In publishing, death be not proud, but it sure can be profitable."

It's been said that for three days after death hair and fingernails continue to grow: the mail doesn't stop, either. Shortly after Random House issued a new edition of *The History of Henry Esmond*, the editors received a letter from a well-known Hollywood agency addressed to the author, William Makepeace Thackeray, who had died a century before. The letter read: "We have read your recent book, *The History of Henry Esmond*, which possesses material adaptable for motion pictures . . . and would like to represent you in the sale of your literary products." The agency added that they would also be interested in any of Thackeray's future stories.

Random House, like most publishers — always looking out for their authors, alive or dead — wrote back thanking the agency for their interest. "[*The History of Henry Esmond*] . . . is a rather crude attempt, I fear, but I am now working on a new novel which will be a natural for the pictures. I am thinking of calling it *Vanity Fair*." The publisher signed the letter, "Sincerely yours, William Makepeace Thackeray."

The students tell me they have read Thackeray; they had to, for their exam. If a writer was dead, asks a young woman, didn't her work have a better chance of being taught at university? "We all have to learn Sylvia Plath;" she goes on to name a dozen more poets who, in my lifetime, have committed suicide and are on the curriculum.

She's right. Death might boost book sales and keep publishers happy, but if fame were to fall only after death, I wasn't in any hurry for the limelight. I was with Woody Allen: I didn't want to achieve immortality through my poetry. I wanted to achieve it through not dying.

WRITER'S RETREAT

❋ When I accepted the short-term writer-in-residence position, it seemed like a good idea. From previous experience I knew what to expect. There would be the older woman who looks me over and says to herself, "Who does she think *she* is?" Worse than that would be the younger one who thinks I *do* know who I am. And in between would be the feminist who, after listening to me expound on the use of metaphor, will say Graeme Gibson told her the opposite last year, the implication being that *he* was right. Graeme speaks in a deep baritone. He's also six foot six.

The bus draws up in front of the building where I am to register, and I unload my travel-worn luggage, thinking of my daughter emptying her piggy bank, asking if she had enough money to come with me. When my host greets me and asks if I have any special needs, I feel inclined to tell her I need to go home. I've always identified with the protagonist in *The Accidental Tourist*, who spends his first day away from home trying to change his ticket so he can fly back earlier. I've already checked into it, though, and there are no trains out of here until tomorrow.

I peruse my class list which, apart from a young girl who is a secondary school student, consists solidly of males. There was another woman registered, from Peru, Indiana, but she has written to cancel. She was planning to bring her new series of poems about flatulence, but when she heard about our recent censorship laws, she was afraid of having her poems seized at the border.

My host hands me a key. My room, she tells me, is clean, In my years of travelling I've learned to distrust two things: anywhere labelled as "paradise," and rooms that are described as "clean."

My room, in the residence of one of Canada's most prominent boys' schools, has been cleaned out for the end of term, except for a couch that's been gutted and a slashed mattress. I don't know if I can rest peacefully staring at RIP on the ceiling, or the swastikas — the graffiti of our country's future leaders — on my walls. I return to the registration desk, where I admit to having developed a special need.

I need to see another room. This one has LOOPY IS A NECROFILIAC improperly spelled on the closet door, along with a detailed definition of what a "necrofiliac" is. I don't want to hang my clothing in Loopy's closet under any conditions, and I go to the desk for a second time, apologizing.

After testing every room, I settle on the first I saw. I'm here to work, after all. I unpack the manuscripts I'm supposed to have read. On top of the pile is a writer of few words, whose complete short story reads, "God lay dying." I make a note that his story lacks conflict and resolution, and suggest he try his hand at writing haiku instead.

Next there is a story by the high school student, about an old lady alone in an old folks' home. She is waiting for her children to visit, although she seldom gets visitors anymore. She feels that life has passed her by. Her only hope is that one of her children will remember to visit today, because it is a special day — her birthday. She is going to be turning forty.

I'm too tired to read anymore, so in the morning I arrange to meet with my students on a one-to-one basis. Private tutorials, I call them, but it's really just a way to buy time. My first appointment, a part-time psychiatric patient, says he wanted to take my workshop because he is "visually oriented" and saw my picture in the brochure. The photo was taken from the back of a book jacket and is more than ten years old. I can see, confronted by me today, he is vaguely disappointed.

My next student tells me he is celebrating his fourteenth day of sobriety. Those aren't consecutive days — it's a ballpark figure for the eighties. The third is a former bank president who claims he lost his ambition and took up writing. He's written two stories, so far, from the point of view of his dog.

I have another special need. Food. When we meet for lunch and the veal cutlet is served, the psych patient feels obliged to give his views on factory farming. The veal calf, he reveals between mouthfuls, is fed on formula that causes severe diarrhea. He lies in his own excrement, choking on the ammonia gases, chained in a darkened room. "It's like a writer," he says, "to use a metaphor."

We will be discussing metaphor later, I tell him. My sober student suggests we adjourn to the pub where we can order a round of vegetarian hamburgers. There we begin our discussion on the creative process.

By the end of the week we're all exchanging addresses and vowing to meet at the bank president's villa in Mexico. By the end of the week, too, my room has become home to me.

When I go home, however, there'll be another period of adjustment. I won't be able to sleep properly without RIP on the ceiling, and it just won't seem the same without swastikas on the walls. Then there'll be all that mail to answer, more invitations to more retreats — which, of course, I'll accept. From previous experience I'll know what to expect, and it will seem like a good idea at the time.

Susan Musgrave

TO BE OR NOT TO BE AN ORGAN DONOR

✳ After being bumped around on the all-night Whisperliner jet service from Seattle, I wished I'd stayed home. I'd accepted a last-minute invitation to judge the Commonwealth Poetry Competition when the Governor General's Award-winning poet had cancelled due to a bad flu. I suspected he had good judgement.

Not that I wasn't qualified. I was a prizewinner myself. In grade three at our school fall fair I had guessed the number of tongue depressors in a jar. I won a doll and named her Maureen Princess Aurora (a romantic even then) before plucking out her eyes and burying her in the sands of Cadboro Bay Beach. Romantics, they say, die young.

As I changed planes in Miami, a sign above the departure lounge doors urged me to BE AN ORGAN DONOR. Hardly the encouragement I needed to continue my journey over the shark-infested waters of the Bermuda Triangle.

With miles to go before I even contemplated sleep, I swallowed my last Gravol. The flight attendant passed out newspapers, and I began reading a front-page article on Miami's seven hundredth homicide of the season. I had reached the back-page obituaries when the plane landed in Trinidad.

I'd been assured by the contest organizers in London that I would be met, but there was no one to greet me except an immigration officer who said his name was Ramón and that he'd like to be my "special friend" in Trinidad.

I told him I was a judge, in Trinidad on business, and he promptly showed me more respect by helping me evade customs. Outside in the humid dark he hailed his brother-in-law's taxi. It didn't *look* like a taxi. I squeezed in.

"The Hilton, please. In St. Augustine," I said, mustering my judgelike authority. Only the whites of my driver's teeth showed in the rearview mirror. "There is no Hilton in St. Augustine," he said. "Only the Scarlet Ibis, and nice persons don't stay there."

I gripped my briefcase, containing my Poetry Competition guidelines. If the organizers had believed the reports of my life, greatly exaggerated, they might well have booked me into the Scarlet Ibis.

"A Hilton, then. Any Hilton," I said, losing my judgelike composure as Ramón's brother-in-law deviated from the main artery, cutting through a cane field. "I am taking you this most scenic route," he replied, accelerating.

Our headlights caught a billboard sign that read HAPPI FLOUR: IT RISES TO THE OCCASION. I collapsed in my seat, remembering what W. H. Auden had said, that "Poetry is small beer. Paying the bills and loving your family is what counts."

Men crouched at the road's edge, waving at us with machetes. My driver indicated points of interest, such as the ditch where a dancer was found only last week with various organs missing. I might not live to pay my overdue Visa bill, or see my family ever again.

By the time I found my letter opener and had figured out which end to use as a weapon, we had emerged from the sugarcane at the Port of Spain Hilton. I overtipped the taxi driver for having had the decency not to dismember me, checked in, and went straight to the bar for my complimentary Corpse Reviver.

In the morning I met with my fellow judges. Our Trinidadian chairman and host apologized for missing my plane, saying his father had been killed in a family matter. Before I could begin to extend my sympathies, he had the contest entries unpacked and was perusing the list of contenders.

We worked through the day, eliminating poets, until we agreed on the prizewinner, a local woman whose themes ranged from oppression to pineapples. Our host couldn't join us for dinner because he had a meeting with his lawyer, so Pamela, the

Australian judge, suggested we leave the hotel and find a better restaurant in town.

"Is it safe," I asked, "for women to go out alone?"

The chairman shook his head. "It is not only the men here who are dangerous. We have one woman who killed a visitor, cut out her heart in the most central part of town." Pamela and I ordered up room service.

The next day the chairman brought the news that our prize-winner had been caught in flagrante delicto, and her husband had set the bed on fire. She had died and become ineligible, so we bumped up our second choice, a Canadian whose themes ranged from snow to beer.

I managed to change my ticket and flee Trinidad the same day. The flight attendant passed out newspapers, and I began reading a front-page account of Miami's seven hundred and thirtieth homicide. "In the final analysis," said one survivor, "this is no way to live."

At the airport, passing under that organ-donor sign, I could feel my heart beating. In the final analysis, I planned to keep things like this.

MAKING PEACE WITH TIME

❋ "I sometimes worry that God has Alzheimer's and has forgotten us." The audience doesn't laugh. Earlier in the day Iraq attacked the environment, spewing oil into the Persian Gulf. Images of oil-soaked cormorants bounce off satellites, spilling over into my lecture on memory and creativity.

Either my sense of humour is too warped or the war is one dirty joke this crowd won't laugh about. As Edmund Gwenn said on his deathbed, dying is easy, comedy is hard.

In the profound silence every spotlight is on me. Anton Chekhov, in his plays, uses a moment of silence broken by the

words, "I remember . . ." The audience sees a woman transformed by her memories and, if it is done well, the audience is
transformed, too.

"I can't remember who," I continue, "but someone once said,
'Nothing is more dangerous to civilization than those who lack
memories.' If any one of our current world leaders were to write
his autobiography, he might do well to entitle it *The Memoirs of an
Amnesiac*."

Finally, a few smiles, so I move on to more serious matters.
My notes tell me to "introduce first poem with anecdote about
great-grandfather." Shell-shocked in the First World War, he
spent the rest of his life worrying about losing his memories. "I
remember . . ." I begin, then all the lights go out.

The audience is transformed. For the first time I hear laughter; they must think the blackout has been orchestrated.

What would Chekhov do? I've forgotten what I was about to
remember. In total darkness I take advantage of the dramatic
value of memory loss and tell the story of Ralph Waldo Emerson, whose memory, as he approached the end of his life, began
to fail. While attending Longfellow's funeral he remarked to a
fellow mourner, "That gentleman had a sweet beautiful soul, but
I have entirely forgotten his name."

Emerson resisted the loss of his "naughty memory" by stick-
ing labels onto everything, describing their function. He identified his plow as "the implement that cultivates the soil." Most
touching was the name he pinned to his umbrella: "the thing that
strangers take away."

My memory hasn't deteriorated to the point where I have to
stick a Post-it on my computer to remember its function, I assure my audience, but if I want to remember something, I have
to write it down. And, lest I forget where I've written it, I entrust
my notes to a computer's memory bank.

Recently, for example, I opened a file named "Forgetfulness."

My first notes read: "Memory is survival. Memory is making peace with time."

I made these notes after reading Timothy Findley's *Inside Memory: Pages from a Writer's Workbook.* Ultimately, Findley says, we *are* what we remember. Without memory we would be unaware that we exist; we would not be able to ask ourselves the question most of us ask every Monday morning on our way to work: "To be or not to be?"

The amphitheatre is so dark that I can't see as far as my hands, let alone my notes for this lecture. I proceed from memory, echoing Findley. "Memory is the means by which most of us retain our sanity. We remember what we have survived, which gives us hope for the future. Memory is the purgative by which we rid ourselves of the present."

"For instance," I say, "right now I'm trying to remember how I've survived past lectures, which might help me purge myself of this present one and give hope for any future." I'm about to qualify that remark with, "These days the future isn't what it used to be," when suddenly I recall what I was about to remember before the lights went out.

"I remember," I tell the audience, now listening attentively, "my great-grandfather, who died because of a war. Death didn't faze him, his nurse told me, but he worried what would become of all his beautiful, and sad, memories. His dying words were, 'Where do all our memories go?'"

"'Poetry is the past that breaks out in our hearts,'" I quote, this time remembering my source (Rilke). It is still dark, so I recite the only poem I know by heart, the one I wrote in memory of my great-grandfather.

"'Where do all our memories go?'" I pause. "I remember . . ." Then the lights come back on.

PART III

The Susan Musgrove?

THE MOVING LOVELINESS OF
HUMAN OCCUPATION

✻ The real estate flyer promised. "'WELCOME HOME,' is what this character cottage will say to *you*. . . . Ideal for the multichild family wishing a single bedroom lifestyle. Walk-in kitchen, semi-attached facilities, only an hour's drive to the nearest road. Needs work, but has AMBIENCE GALORE!"

Of course I bought the dump. I identified with it, from the moment my foot went through the hole in the punky front porch.

Writers, whose homes are usually also their workplaces, often give identity to, and are identified with, their dwellings, says Witold Rybczynski, the Montreal architect. Samuel Clemens described his Connecticut home as having "a heart and soul and eyes to see with." Robert Louis Stevenson spent his last years living in Polynesia in the "beautiful, shining, windy house" he built himself.

My house was built by a local poet. Winds gust down the 190-foot Douglas fir growing through our living room; the tree's roots form our only foundations. Rats first took refuge in our walls during the Great Depression. They lined their nests with the newspapers used for insulation.

Carl Jung described a house as an extension of the unconscious, "a kind of representation of one's innermost thoughts." Since we moved in, three years ago, I haven't had time to think about my thoughts; I've been too busy fighting with the extension ladder. A day hasn't passed when we haven't had to tear down a wall, replace a rotten floorboard, or patch a leaky ceiling. When our multichild family outgrew a single bedroom lifestyle, we simply added on, so that the house has also grown around us. It has also grown to embody our personalities.

"We live in a house, and in the process we make it alive," Rybczynski writes. If we think of buildings as clothes, he says, a house should be like a worn and carefully patched jacket that takes the shape of its wearer over time and becomes a sort of second skin.

Houses should shelter daydreaming, Rybczynski also says, "which is to say that our houses take life in our imaginations. That is why the places that people have fashioned for themselves are more touching than those — no matter how splendid — that others have made for them."

I recall these words as I drive my daughter to visit a new friend. My old beater barely makes it up the hill to Eagle's Nest Estates where there are no longer any trees for the eagles to nest in. Instead there are mock Georgian ranchettes designed for homeowners who think "upkeep" means turning a key in a lock. "Mum," cries my daughter, "look at all the beautiful houses where *real* people live!"

How can I tell her, without sounding judgemental, that it's quite the opposite? Our dump may not be dripping in elegance like these key-ready ranchettes, but it exhibits something, to me, that is more precious, what Rybczynski calls "the moving loveliness of human occupation." Our house, with a real heart and soul and real eyes to see with, is evidence of how human beings can transform a place, "not by grand design but by the small celebrations of everyday life." It may not be anyone else's idea of a "dream home," but our

Susan Musgrave

house *contains* our dreams. "We have things that other people don't have," I say softly.

"Yeah," she replies, "like rats in our walls." She jumps out at a mock Tudor gatehouse and waves to her friend, waiting beside a heated pool that wouldn't even fit on our property. Which reminds me, it's time to fill the old bathtub on the lawn — for the children to paddle in now that the weather's heated up.

Home again, I make my way out of the rain and up the wobbly front porch steps. I don't have to search for our front door key — it's been in the lock ever since it got stuck there. I don't have to search for my husband, either. Every time it rains I can find him up the ladder with a bucket of roofing tar. He's promised to have those porch steps nailed down today, too, before *The Journal* crew arrives to film my review of Rybczynski's new book, *The Most Beautiful House in the World*.

I've barely hung my coat on its finishing nail when my daughter phones, begging me to pick her up. She wants to show her friend *our* beautiful house. As we talk, I feel a steady drip-drip-drip down my neck.

My husband sticks his head in the door as I stick a saucepan under the drip. "This time I've fixed that leak for good!" he pronounces. Welcome home, I think.

WHAT'S *NOT* IN A NAME

❋ On Christmas Eve two years ago I was reading my way through a stack of baby-name books. I had gone from biblical to New Age, but nothing seemed to fit the overdue lump inside me.

At the bottom of the pile I found *What NOT to Name the Baby*. The authors, Roger Price and Leonard Stern, contend that names — not heredity, environment, television, or lack of fibre — are responsible for our inept personalities. Until a baby is given a name, say the authors, it continues to be a dampish noisy lump with little personality and, to the objective observer, not even any sex. Their theory is that once the baby has a name, society begins to treat it as if it had the type of personality the name implies, and the child grows up to fit the name.

"Take myself," says Price. "As a result of being named ROGER, I wore glasses when I was nine, which made me look studious, and I made the best grades in school." If he'd been named NICK, he maintains, he would have had twenty-twenty vision and instead of studying would have been playing marbles for keeps in the school basement.

In fiction, where every character (like every person) is the embodiment of a complicated philosophical way of looking at the world, a name, I knew, could be a strong clue to a character's personality. "There was a boy called Eustace Clarence Scrubb, and he almost deserved it," wrote C. S. Lewis in *The Voyage of the Dawn Treader*. On the other hand, Scarlett O'Hara was *undeserving* of the name Margaret Mitchell gave her in an early draft of *Gone with the Wind*. Mitchell had named her heroine PANSY.

"A name is a kind of face," wrote Thomas Fuller, summing up the way most of us think, not only about our own names, but about those of other people. We feel as possessive of our names as we do of our reflections in a mirror.

For instance, I once introduced a former husband by my present husband's name. To hide his hurt feelings he retaliated with that overused line from *Auntie Mame*, "You can call me anything, just don't call me late for dinner."

It was an innocent mistake, I assured him. I had so many names to keep track of in my life! But change *my* name by so much as a single letter, and my character — my way of looking at the world — changes, too. Who but a physically careless, insensitive boor would be guilty of asking me, "Are you *the* Susan Musgrove?"

My surname, Musgrave, has always been the strongest clue to who I am (reverse it and you get "Grave-muse"). Over the years, though, I'd grown used to my given name. And since having read a British survey where SUSAN was voted the name with the most sex appeal, I've actually been able to live with it.

But when I looked up my name in *What NOT to Name the Baby*, the authors gave it a different interpretation. "SUSAN organizes things and bakes cookies." I thought of other writers I knew and found more exceptions. "RUDY is fat, wears a pinky ring and uses terrible language" didn't, for a minute, describe the writer Rudy Wiebe, who is thin and eschews jewellery. "JUNE dresses to call attention to her shoulders" was not June Callwood.

"You will at times see flagrant exceptions to the conclusions expressed here," say Price and Stern. "These exceptions merely prove the validity of our theory."

What NOT to name the baby became an awesome responsibility. Should I risk naming my son GAYLORD and trust that he's a not-so-flagrant exception and doesn't grow up to be a "bridal consultant"? By calling my daughter EUPHEMIA, am I ensuring she'll become "a homely little kid who bites"?

A week after my dampish lump was barking *my* name over the Fisher-Price monitor, she was still nameless. In desperation we settled on SOPHIE, because my eldest daughter said she *seemed* like a SOPHIE and not because the name wasn't popular enough to be listed in *What NOT to Name the Baby*.

On January 4 SOPHIE (which, in classical baby-name books, means "wisdom") will be five. Just as a ROSE is not always a ROSE, SOPHIE is more of a TOBY. According to Price and Stern's theory, she will change. Chances are she'll grow up to be the kind of person her name sounds like she ought to be.

Then again there's always a possibility that, like another couple on Christmas Eve two thousand years ago, we chose the wrong name. Away in a manger, MARY and JOSEPH called their newborn babe JEHOSHEA. JEHOSHEA, according to Rabbi Saul Kraft, was an immigrant name, which is why it was changed to JESUS.

THE GIFT

�֎ I used to be paranoid. Last week, for instance, when my signal lights weren't working and I found myself trailing a squad car to town, I convinced myself that the police were actually following *me*. I had to lose them. I slowed until they were out of sight, then took an alternate route to my doctor's office.

My doctor said that paranoia, like jealousy, was simply another form of intuition. I'd been gifted with strong intuitions, I knew, and drove straight to the garage to get my indicators fixed.

Late Sunday afternoon I sent my husband and daughter to Sidney for boneless chicken breasts. Really, it was an excuse — I wanted some time alone. It was raining; I told them to drive carefully and not to hurry back. Five minutes after they left, I was standing at the window, waiting for them to return.

It seemed to be raining harder. The road looked slick; would the tires grip? I set to work making the chocolate chip surprises I'd been promising all weekend.

I had the first batch in the oven when I heard the siren. Racing to the window, I saw a police car making a U-turn right in front of our house. He sped off, lights flashing, toward town.

My family had been gone for thirty-five minutes. It didn't take that long to buy boneless chicken breasts at Thrifty's unless, of course, Thrifty's didn't have any and they'd had to go farther afield, to Safeway, for example. I'd decided I'd give them another ten minutes before I really started worrying, when a fire truck streaked past, followed by an ambulance.

If you want peace, prepare for war — that's my motto. At once I imagined my car, with the two people I loved more than life itself, trapped inside. How soon would anybody notify me? If the glove compartment had been spared, someone would find registration papers, and even though my address had changed and I hadn't bothered to inform Motor Vehicles, I still had the same telephone number.

Susan Musgrave

90

Four fifty-five. I checked my cookies and went to wait by the telephone. I'd never realized how lonely an empty booster seat could look on a chair, or a pair of trousers with the top button missing. My husband had been asking me for months to sew that button on, "When you have a moment."

Living alone, I'd have moments. No, I thought, I would take my own life rather than live on without my family. I would hurl myself off the cliff that very evening.

The cliff was across the road. But when I looked, I saw that the tide was unusually low. I saw a family clamming at the water's edge. If I were to kill myself tonight, I would have to hurl myself off the mud flats and spoil that family's outing.

Five o'clock. Maybe the police wouldn't phone but would send someone personally, in which case they would go to the wrong address. Oh, why hadn't I informed Motor Vehicles when I moved? Rather than wait the days it would probably take for them to track me down, I decided to take the plunge. It took a lot of guts to call the RCMP and ask, "Have there been any casualties in the Safeway parking lot this evening?"

"No accidents," the Colwood detachment, which is what you get when you call the police in Sidney, informed me, "At least none that have been reported."

None that had been reported. I hung up, no happier than before, and stared at the treacherous road. I just knew it; I should have had my tires rotated. My mechanic had called me a worrywart the last time, so I hadn't wanted to mention it.

"I have suffered a great many catastrophes in my life," Mark Twain wrote. "Most of them have never happened." I was trying to convince myself that nothing might have happened this time, either, that it was simply "another form of intuition" taking hold of my better judgement, when the brown Accord slowed and pulled into the drive. My husband and daughter emerged alive. "Something's burning," my daughter said as she came bounding through the front door laden with packages.

Musgrave Landing

I took the charred surprises out of the oven and put the frozen chicken wings — all they'd been able to get — in the sink to thaw. My husband had bought a record, one he'd wanted for Christmas, and I listened to a cut called "Mothers of the Disappeared" while my daughter told me they'd been all over Sidney trying to find something to cheer me up. But it wasn't until I broke open the box of small heart-shaped chocolates she'd bought in a post-Valentine's sale that I burst into tears properly.

"See," said my daughter, looking knowingly at my husband. "I told you I knew how to make her happy."

THROUGH THICK AND THIN

✳ My eight-year-old daughter finds me in the hammock struggling to read a tome that weighs more than both of us. "Mum," she says, "that's a totally thick book."

She's not the first to have made such a remark about *A History of the Decline and Fall of the Roman Empire*. The Duke of Gloucester, when presented with the second volume, said, as the author laid his life's work on the table, "Another damn'd thick, square book. Always scribble, scribble, scribble! Eh! Mr. Gibbon?"

My daughter takes Edward Gibbon's masterpiece off my hands and sets it on the ground to serve as a stool. She's brought a magazine for each of us. She keeps the thick fashion number promising SEX IN THE BRAIN: HOW TO BLOW YOUR MATE'S MIND, handing me the literary supplement. In it there's an interview with John Steinbeck about the advantages of fat books.

Every book I've read lately has been fat. I've skimmed both volumes of *War and Peace* (I agree with Woody Allen — it's about Russia) and have managed to speed-read a couple of massive bestsellers — the kind where the main character doesn't say hello until page 546. Next on my summer reading hit list is *Ulysses*.

Susan Musgrave

According to Steinbeck, I'm no different from most readers, who have the impression that a big book is more important and has more authority than a short book. His explanation for this is that the human mind is bee-stung with a thousand little details from taxes to war worry and the price of meat. Now, he says, we must think of a book as a wedge driven into our personal life; a short book would be in and out quickly. A long book, on the other hand, drives in very slowly and remains there for a while. Instead of cutting and leaving, it allows the mind to rearrange itself to fit around the wedge.

Steinbeck carries the analogy even further. "When the quick wedge is withdrawn, the tendency of the mind is to heal itself quickly, exactly as it was before the attack. With the long book the healing has been warped around the shape of the wedge so that when the wedge is finally withdrawn and the book set down, the mind cannot ever be quite what it was before. Living with [the book] longer has given it greater force."

But what about a short story by Edgar Allan Poe? Whose mind hasn't been warped around one of those? And who has *ever* healed after reading Raymond Carver? If Steinbeck's theory is true, this means any long book — the 38,000-page official manual of the Internal Revenue Service, for instance — would make a bigger impression than a collection of stories by Alice Munro. I'm more inclined to side with E. M. Forster, who said that one always tends to overpraise a long book simply because one has got through it, or with the editor who first said, "In every fat book there is a thin book trying to get out."

These days, though, thick books are the height of fashion. According to surveys, North Americans want fat books and thin women. While this may explain the glut of diet books on the market, it may also explain why history's thinnest book, Elbert Hubbard's *Essay on Silence*, which consists of empty pages, has never made it to the bestseller list.

I try to make sense of Steinbeck's wedge theory for my

daughter, who thinks big books are a big bore. "If you think they're so rad," she challenges, glancing up from her magazine, "why don't you try to write one?"

Her question has a familiar ring. Recently, after giving a poetry reading, I had all my slim volumes laid out for sale on the table when a woman asked if I'd ever written any "real" books. By "real" she meant fat, blockbuster-type novels.

It's not that I don't *want* to write big books, I explain to my daughter, or that I deliberately set out to make thin ones. They just grow that way. I write 38,000 pages in order to get three. It takes me a long time to make my work short.

An itch for scribbling has taken possession of me. I plot out loud the possible ways of expanding my latest three-pager into 38,000, but my daughter isn't listening. Her mind is on other things, such as an article entitled "Natural Bust Enlargement with Total Mind Power: How to Use the Other 90 Percent of Your Mind to Increase the Size of Your Breasts," and waiting for them to happen.

I don't want bigger breasts. But substitute "book" for "bust" and it might be what I need to write my bestseller.

INVENTING "FUNNY WOMANNESS"

✳ "How many feminists does it take to screw in a light bulb?" the joke goes. The correct answer is five. One to screw in the light bulb, two to discuss the violation of the socket, and two to wish secretly they were that socket.

According to Evelyn Edson (*Iris: A Journal About Women*, Fall 1988), the *real* answer is "That's not funny." The light bulb joke is a prime example of sexist humour, but when feminists don't laugh they get the reputation of being humourless. Yet "it is not so obvious that feminists *should* have a sense of humour," she maintains. "Humour can help us deal with difficult situations, but may weaken the will to change them by ridiculing all effort."

Not so, says the cartoonist Lynda Barry. She believes humour *can* change your point of view. *If you can laugh* at an intelligent woman with a college degree wishing she had bigger breasts or convinced that no one will love her because she has five stretch marks on her left thigh, *then you can begin to change the way you see things.*

When Barry was in college, her goal was to be the most depressed person on the planet. She thought depression meant that everyone would take her seriously and she'd have the most boyfriends. She found an "adequately depressed man," and they were depressed together until he met a blonde who was happy. At that point Barry threw aside her depression in favour of laughing.

Edson argues that women smile too much, trying to be accommodating in social situations where indignation or even rage would be more honest. Humour can be used to *defuse* anger and undermine action. Successful revolutionaries, she points out, are not usually noted for their love of fun.

Lynda Barry doesn't think laughter can be dangerous, because it's a barometer of a belief system. So if you laugh at a racist or sexist joke, the laughing is without blame. But it should make you take a serious look at your belief system.

Laugh especially at things you should be ashamed to laugh at, she says. Barry's cartoons often address the more ridiculous obsessions of North American women, our deeply entrenched feelings about body image, for instance. In "Four Ways to Change Your Profile," parodying the makeovers featured monthly in women's magazines, she depicts a woman "lending bland eyes an air of oriental flair" by twisting a coat hanger around her head.

"As soon as I can laugh about something, I have power over it," says Barry. "When I laugh at it, I see what a self-pitying, ridiculous creature I've become over the slightest thing. I think that in certain ways you can work up the same anxiety over large pores as you can over nuclear holocaust. It's a shameless fact."

Traditionally women comedians have relied on a self-deprecating and ingratiating sense of humour, casting themselves as stereotypes and pitting themselves against one another. "I was in a beauty contest once," quipped Phyllis Diller. "I not only came in last but I was hit in the mouth by Miss Congeniality." Roseanne Barr, in bringing feminist humour to prime time, says she had to create a whole new category of comedy called "funny womanness" because "there wasn't any language to name women's experience and make it funny to men *and* women."

Which raises another point — is there a female sense of humour as opposed to a typically male one? Little research has been done on the varying reactions of men and women to humour, Evelyn Edson tells us, but a study reported at the International Conference of Humour and Laughter in the late seventies examined whether male chauvinist jokes appealed more to attractive or unattractive women (the scholars didn't say why they chose this particular line of research). At first the researchers ranked the women on an attractiveness scale of one to four, but when this method was criticized as being too subjective, they substituted an *objective* criterion — breast size. Edson reports that the "unattractive" women were more amused by the sexist jokes — "at any rate, they smiled harder."

Humour comes out of self-confidence. In the last two decades we've begun to see the emergence of more humorists with a straight-ahead feminist angle. Artists like Roseanne Barr and Lynda Barry are not afraid to laugh at men; they're not afraid of showing women how to laugh at themselves, either.

So next time you make yourself suicidal over a stretch mark, try laughing. If that doesn't help, do what I do. Screw in a dimmer light bulb.

Susan Musgrave

OTHER POSSIBILITIES

✳ "Art cannot be achieved by those for whom anything else matters more," writes Carolyn Heilbrun, author of *Reinventing Womanness*. "Art, like passion, is not a part-time occupation."

In my twenties I would have bought that romantic notion. I then believed domesticity and the creative process were incompatible, that in order to be a real artist you needed a remote cabin, paper, food, and a part-time lover to provide suffering.

"Listen to this!" As my husband struggles to get our baby into her corduroy Snugli, I read: "'The real artist is engaged in a full-time struggle, which is harder for women, among other reasons, because they do not have wives.'"

He secures the Snugli to his chest so the baby can watch him do last night's dishes, and sows a handful of rolled oats into the pressure cooker. "Who hasn't got enough wives?"

"'Most of the great women writers,'" I keep reading, "'have been unmarried. Those who have written in the state of wedlock have done so in peaceful kingdoms guarded by devoted husbands. Few have had children.'"

My husband adjusts the heat under the pressure cooker. "I thought you were going to your office."

Brenda Ueland, in *If You Want to Write*, has this advice for mothers: "If you would shut your door against the children for an hour a day and say: 'Mother is working on her five-act tragedy in blank verse!' you would be surprised how they would respect you."

I call to my oldest daughter as I pass the television. "Mother's going out to work on her — "

"Is breakfast ready?" she shouts back over Garfield *and* the explosion in the kitchen.

"Dad's working on it."

In the peaceful kingdom of my office I curl up with my book. Heilbrun cites Virginia Woolf as one of the lucky ones who found a nurturing man; Woolf knew that women with diapers to change and meals to arrange could not be artists, as well. To be truly an artist, she said, is to retain control of one's destiny, and women struggling their way to a sense of identity through the encircling meshes of domesticity were not artists, but victims.

For the women who did manage to write, the options were limited. Death and marriage were the only two possible ends for women in novels and were, frequently, the same end, Heilbrun writes. So full of anxiety were women before the current women's movement that, when imagining other possibilities of female destinies, they went to great pains to conceal their authorial identities. (George Sand, for instance, became a male impersonator.) It's hard now to conceive of certain subjects being considered "unwomanly," but it wasn't so long ago that Charlotte Bronte's closest friends were describing her novels as coarse and unbecoming in their presentation of passion.

I boot up my computer and get to work. These days women can write openly about intimacy; when Anna Quindlen, columnist for the *New York Times*, says, "another year has gone by and still the Nobel prize has not been awarded to the inventors of the Snugli baby carrier," it's because she sees her life as interacting with her art. So does Sharon Olds make poetry out of her father's snoring, or the right way to insert a diaphragm.

Neither Quindlen nor Olds gave up writing when they became mothers. A passion for writing never decreases, just as when your second child is born you don't love your first any the less.

"When I was twenty-five," Quindlen writes, "I always felt as if a bus were coming around the corner with my name on its front bumper, and that I'd damn well better have spent the day working on a good opening sentence for my obit. Now it seems as if there are so many years ahead. . . . and if I get the forty additional years statisticians say are likely coming to me, I could fit in one, maybe two new lifetimes. Sad that only one of those lifetimes can include being the mother of young children."

Susan Musgrave

98

Today's writers — men *and* women — know that art *can* be achieved by those for whom other things, like family, matter more. When Ken Kesey, author of *One Flew over the Cuckoo's Nest*, was asked why he hadn't published a book in many years, he replied, "I felt like you can write forever, but you have a short time to raise a family."

Now I'm really cooking. I'm beginning to feel as if I could write forever when my husband brings tea. It's his way of telling me it's my turn to take the kids.

My daughter trails in, toting the baby. "'But-you-have-a-short-time-to-raise-a-family,'" she reads aloud over my shoulder. "Mum," she says, "you've been out here all morning. Is that *all* you've written?"

It's time to cook lunch. Passion, I've learned, can be divided without being diminished. I hug my daughters and hit SAVE THIS FILE.

BORN TO MAUL

✿ The walls of my house are lined with books. When visitors ask, "Have you read all these?" I point out the cracked spines, the tatty, dust jackets, the stains, and marginalia.

The recent toothmarks, though, aren't mine. Nor am I responsible for the shreds of *Esquire*'s "Summer Reading Bash Issue" all over the living room, or the chewed-up *Utne Reader*s and spit-out *Brick*s. Every one of Alan Fotheringham's pictures in *Maclean's* has been defaced with a Crayola.

My husband — who rose early with the baby — looks up from his newspaper. "It says here a recycling depot is making a deal with funeral homes to use shredded magazines for coffin linings," he tells me when I toss him a couple of chewed *Utne*s. That the walls of my coffin could be lined with shredded Fotheringhams seems fitting.

Musgrave Landing

I leave the baby sampling back issues of *Gourmet* in the kitchen and follow chunks of *The Omnipotent Child* all the way to my office. She's been busy in here also and has done her best to destroy Irish novelist and columnist Flann O'Brien's (aka Myles na Gopaleen) *The Best of Myles.*

I assure myself that this book-mauling phase will pass as I start taping *Myles* back together again. Only one column, headed "Buchandling," has survived unchewed: "Recently I visited the house of a newly-married acquaintance — a man of great wealth and vulgarity," it begins. "When he had set about buying bedsteads, tables, and chairs, it occurred to him to buy also a library."

Myles na Gopaleen did not know whether this man could read or not, but "some savage faculty of observation told him that most respectable and estimable people usually had a lot of books in their houses," so he bought several bookcases and paid someone to fill them. ("Get plenty of snappy red and green books with lots of gilt lettering.") When Myles next visited the house, he noticed that none of the books had ever been opened.

"'When I am settled down properly,' said his friend, 'I'll have to catch up on my reading.'"

Myles has an idea: why should a wealthy person like this be put to the trouble of pretending to read at all? If he wants to be suspected of reading books, why couldn't a professional book handler go in and suitably maul his library for so much per shelf? Such a person, if properly trained, could make a fortune.

My baby doesn't need training. She can alter a book in so few seconds that anybody looking at it would conclude its owner has lived, dined, and slept with it for months.

I read on. Myles suggests four categories in which books could be mauled, starting with "Popular Handling," where each volume would be well and truly fondled, with four pages dog-eared and a tram ticket inserted in each as a forgotten bookmark. In "Premier Handling" each volume would be thoroughly

Susan Musgrave

mauled, eight pages dog-eared, and a leaflet in French on the works of Victor Hugo left to mark a place.

For the very wealthy non-brow who wants to appear high-brow, there is "De Luxe Handling." Each volume will be savagely mauled, the spines of the trade paperbacks damaged so as to give the impression their owner carries them around in his pocket, a passage in every volume underlined in red ink, and an old theatre program left as a forgotten bookmark. Not less than thirty volumes will be treated with old coffee or whiskey stains and many will be inscribed with forged signatures of the authors.

And finally, "Handling Superb," or "Le Traitement Superbe" — "the dearest of them all, though far cheaper than dirt when you consider the amount of prestige you will gain in the eyes of your friends." This category includes all features of the others, and more! An appropriate eye-catching phrase such as "How true, how true," "Nonsense," or "Yes, but cf. Homer, Od, iii, 151" will be scrawled in the margins and not less than six volumes will be inscribed with forged messages of affection and gratitude from the author of each work, i.e., "From your devoted friend and follower, K. Marx."

I accent the last category with a fluorescent Quick Reference Marker. I can picture my daughter just doing what she does best — bending, bashing, chewing, and gnawing, then, Crayola in fist, scribbling, "Quite, but Boussuet in his *Discours sur l'histoire universelle* has already established the same and given much more forceful explanations," in the margin of some capitalist's *Das Kapital.* She'll make a killing.

'TIS THE SEASON

❄ My daughter was hanging little wooden children by their necks from the tree. "Christmas is coming, the goose is getting fat, please put a penny in an old man's hat," she chanted until I felt like strangling *her*. I bolted a fire extinguisher to the wall and suggested she put on a Christmas album.

Before I could say the Mormon Tabernacle Choir she had Michael Jackson carolling "Smooth Criminal," which reminded me my husband was being awfully quiet.

I found him decking our entrance hall with sprigs of holly. I told him the berries were going to drop off and get trodden into our new wool carpet if the baby didn't choke on them first. She'd already made salad out of the poinsettia.

In the kitchen, by the wood stove, I sat down and almost wept. I could no longer ignore the Christmas baking list my daughter had made for me. She was insisting we leave shortbread for Santa "like normal people do"; last year, she'd pointed out, he'd left a boot print in my Middle Eastern Eggplant Dip.

My husband must have heard me stoking the fire with recipe books because he climbed off his ladder and fixed me a buttered rum. He also gave me a "small pre-Christmas present."

"You shouldn't have!" I was about to cry. But when I saw the paper bag I knew it couldn't be the twenty-volume Oxford English Dictionary at $2,500 I'd been hoping for. I bit my tongue and peeled the price tag off *The Portable Curmudgeon*.

It didn't take me long to figure out why my husband had chosen the book. "Curmudgeons are mockers and debunkers," the author says in his introduction. Many of them had unhappy childhoods and grew into neurotic, reclusive, self-centred adults. Besides being inexpensive, the book was dedicated to "Nobody."

"Thanks for thinking of me," I said, opening the door for my husband, who was dragging the ladder after him. He disappeared off the porch with a string of coloured lights in his teeth. I wasn't about to watch him fall and break his neck scaling the chimney, so I went back inside, grinding a few holly berries into the carpet just so I could say "I told you so."

I set *The Portable Curmudgeon* aside on a heap of greeting cards that had been arriving since Thanksgiving. I still hadn't mailed my cards, with "Seasonally Adjusted Greetings" on them, nor had I posted my daughter's letter to Santa. I had to steam it open and find out how much Christmas was going to set me back this year.

And I had real work to do. Christmas might be coming, the goose might be getting fat, but if I didn't finish my column, my editor wouldn't put a loonie in my hat. I didn't have time to start enjoying myself simply because the calendar told me there were five shopping days left until Christmas.

Besides, in my own neurotic, reclusive, self-centred way I was happy. And, as Quentin Crisp says, happy people do not need festivity.

The cure for Christmas, he advises, is to ignore it. So that evening, while my husband sat down to play Silly Safari with my daughter — a game sent to me by its inventors after they read my column on how I found board games about as entertaining as those blow-in subscription forms that fall out of magazines — I put the baby to sleep and went to my office to work. But with an army of unwrapped Teenage Mutant Ninja Turtles staring up at me from the floor, all I could do was snarl at the season's excesses, thrust upon us by shopkeepers and the press. "On its own merits Christmas would wither and shrivel in the fiery breath of universal hatred," George Bernard Shaw said. In my books even Shaw could get sentimental at Christmas.

I was sitting down to wrap the mutants when I remembered my daughter's letter. "Dear Santa," it began, "I don't waunt any prasints this year. I waunt you to give my mum some nice mony so she dosi'nt have to werk. I waunt her to play games with me instaed. P.S. I *would* like some tenage moutint ninga tertles."

When I finished my column, I went back inside. My husband had cleaned half the berry stains off the carpet and my daughter had plugged in the Christmas tree lights. I sniffed the air. Nothing was burning.

They were starting another game of Silly Safari. I pushed the remains of the poinsettia aside and sat down to read the rules. Anything to avoid making shortbread.

COPING WITH REALITY

✷ "I hate to advocate drugs, alcohol, violence or insanity," says Hunter S. Thompson, "but they've always worked for me." If a Canadian journalist wrote *that*, he could be charged under the Criminal Code with "promoting literature for illicit drug use."

So far this little-known law seems only to have been levelled against "how-to" literature. Leaflets on growing marijuana hydroponically have gone underground. But what if, a few dark years from now, the law's definition of "literature" chooses to include poetry and fiction? Once a law's on the books — like the War Measures Act — it's a law lying in ambush.

Drugs have always worked for the protagonist of my new novel. She smokes pot because it has a soothing effect on her central nervous system. She and her husband snort cocaine on Friday night when the kids are sleeping and drop acid on their anniversary to "keep their priorities in perspective." They are well-informed, productive people who like to get high.

Ronald Siegel, a UCLA psychopharmacologist, argues that the motivation to achieve an altered mood or consciousness is a "fourth drive" — as much a part of the human condition, and as important to most other species, as sex, thirst, and hunger. During the Vietnam War, he says, water buffalo were observed nibbling on opium poppies more often than they naturally do. This was similar to what American soldiers were doing with heroin.

People use drugs, from caffeine to heroin, for one purpose, Siegel believes. "They are medicating themselves. They are changing their mood. They are changing the way they feel."

The way most people feel about our present government you'd think our leaders would welcome *any* mood change. Besides, drugs create a billion-dollar-a-year prison "industry," marijuana smugglers provide thousands of hours of on-the-job training for Canada's Coast Guard, and cocaine has converted millions of Canadians to the metric system.

"Reality is a crutch for those who can't cope with drugs," said Lily Tomlin. Instead of coping with drugs *or* reality the government blows another smoke screen in our faces. They reduce complex social problems into, simply, drug problems, and use the "War on Drugs" to divert our attention from the real issues.

On the surface it appears as if the media is fighting the government's war; in fact, no one promotes illicit drugs so well. An all-too-exciting magazine cover in the eighties, for example, was the map of South America on which a mound of cocaine was being chopped into lines with an American Express gold card. More recently we've been introduced to crack. As Bruce Alexander, a Simon Fraser psychology professor, writes in the *Vancouver Sun*, alluring tales are told in Britain of riches to be made peddling this highly euphoric, affordable, "most addictive drug on earth." If crack doesn't take off in the U.K., he says, it won't be the fault of the publicity campaign run by the media.

Last month we got literature from DAWN (Drug Awareness Week Network). Instead of more propaganda and over-dramatized examples of what can happen to drug users, this year "warm fuzzy bookmarks" were handed out to "help people feel good about themselves."

I was buying a mickey of something that would help me feel even better about myself when I saw the Drug Awareness Week poster. With alcohol having killed 125,000 people last year (National Institute on Drug Abuse figures), tobacco 346,000, cocaine 2,000, and marijuana 75 (those 75 were also bungie jumping at the time), what better place for awareness to dawn than in a government liquor store! I put the bottle back and went next door to the Drug Mart for extra-strength Tylenol instead.

My reality being what it is most days (violent outbursts over approaching deadlines, and constant insanity) my new novel may take time. But if the book is published and I find myself in the prisoner's box because my characters don't say "no to drugs," I'll be in high company. I've made a list of writers from William Burroughs to Tom Wolfe who, for what they've written about drugs, would have to be booked also.

The truth is, you can tell people the truth (cocaine can make you feel good; marijuana can make you happy) and they're not going to rush out to mainline their Child Benefit cheques. I hate to advocate the truth, but . . .

Go ahead, Attorney General. Make my day.

MUSGRAVE LANDING

❋ I admit I regard flying as most fighter pilots regarded the Second World War — just long periods of boredom interspersed with moments of sheer terror. For escapism I've picked up the last copy of *Famous Last Words* at the airport bookstore.

"Goodbye, everybody," says my mother sitting next to me as the 767 pushes back from the ramp. Those were Hart Crane's departing words, too, as he leaped from the deck of a ship in mid-ocean.

My mother toys with her lighter, anxious for the NO SMOK-ING sign to be extinguished. But when the captain interrupts the piped-in music he says we will be able to enjoy a smoke-free environment en route to Toronto. My mother puts her lighter away and starts fuming.

"For God's sake, you have to die of something," she says, rummaging through her purse for a Lifesaver. "Death would be comparatively pleasant, as opposed to some ordeals, I mean. Like living. For five hours without a cigarette."

I remind her that secondhand smoke is dangerous to people's health, using Saki, the great short story writer, as an example.

"Put that bloody cigarette out!" were Saki's famous last words, moments before he was killed by a sniper's bullet.

"This isn't World War II," my mother retaliates. "It's supposed to be Hospitality Service."

The bullying music grows louder as the plane taxis into position for takeoff. Then: "Ladies and gentlemen, this is your captain again. With any luck we should be in the air momentarily." *With any luck? Momentarily?* To someone who takes words literally this sounds ominous.

We hurtle up the runway. "They're playing 'Nearer My God to Thee,'" says my mother. It's a strange choice for takeoff.

We're airborne. I have my first moment of sheer terror when the wheels retract. Then boredom sets in and I return to my book. Rousseau's dying words, "I go to see the sun for the last time," appear in front of my eyes as the 767 breaks through the clouds into the blue, unappeasable sky.

I grit my teeth and relax as we climb to our cruising altitude. My mother, in lieu of smoking, has her hands clenched in prayer. I don't pray when I'm on the ground and refuse to alter my standards simply because I'm in a life-threatening situation. The idea that one should use God as a form of oxygen mask or life jacket seems to me hypocritical.

The captain, although he is expecting some turbulence, suggests we sit back and enjoy the view. Personally I don't enjoy anything at 41,000 feet. "This is utter hell," I say as we bump eastward over the mountains. I hate to think these might be *my* last words.

"Amen," says my mother, inhaling another Lifesaver. "Dad used to hold my hand whenever it got rough."

I take her hand. My father died four years ago.

"I always feel closer to Dad when I'm up here," she says quietly. Then, when the turbulence is over, she says, "I wonder what hell is really like, anyway."

The flight attendant moves through the cabin distributing

complimentary wine. My mother, with her mask on, can't decide between the red or white. I ask what we are having.

"There's a choice of chicken or pork," the flight attendant informs me. "But you don't get a choice. It's pork."

Something in my look makes her hasten to explain. "You see in First Class they have a choice. If there are any leftovers, then we can offer them to you in Hospitality."

"Leftovers!" I hear myself cry. My mother, who has heard the same cry all her life, sighs with the flight attendant. I raise my voice in protest. "Leftovers!" I picture plates of little chicken bones picked clean by First Class vultures.

"But the peasants — how do the peasants die!" I cry, quoting the dying Tolstoy. It works. They bring chicken.

Hours later it's dark and a new moon is rising over Lake Ontario. I read of the Chinese poet Li Po, who fell out of a boat and was drowned when he tried to embrace the moon's reflection. His last words are untranslatable.

There comes a final moment of terror when I hear the plane's engine change pitch. When it's clear to me we're only going down, I reach to embrace my mother.

"We must be landing," I say, relieved.

"Famous last words," says my mother.

THE ART OF GETTING THERE

❊ Planning a vacation? A degree in psychology might help, plus a crash course in stress management. Relaxing, after all, is a major cause of stress; it's right up there with fear of dying in a plane wreck.

But I've promised my mother and my daughter a vacation. "Advance attention to your personality is crucial," states the first self-help book I pull from the library shelves. Before going on a vacation, the doctor-authors say, it's a good idea to know *who* you are. (They include a chart, which tells me I'm in the "finiteness of life and urgency of time" cycle. Isn't everyone?)

I know one thing about myself: I crave risk, as long as it's not life-threatening. If I'd paid attention to this conservative side of my nature before spelunking in bear country on our last vacation, my daughter's father and I might still be undivorced.

Before setting out, the authors advise, it is important to have a destination. My daughter doesn't care where we end up as long as our hotel has a VCR, and no grizzlies. I want excitement; my mother will settle for paradise. Luckily I have a travel agent who can satisfy all our desires. Shelagh at Alladin books us a "Flying Carpet Tour" to Disneyland.

But for the doctor-authors, knowing *where* you're going isn't enough. Now I'm supposed to ask myself *why*. Am I looking for a rest, or "One Last Fling at Self-Improvement"? (I'm in that life cycle category, too.) Is it a "Cultural Quest," or do I want "Brief Sexual Encounters of an Intensely Satisfying Kind"?

I won't find any of the above at Disneyland. As I pay for the nonrefundable airline tickets, I have second thoughts about going *anywhere* this summer. Why not stay home and avoid relaxing altogether? The book calls this "Terrors of the Week Before."

Doubt, depression, despair — these are all normal states of mind, the doctors assure me, for anyone going on a vacation. To avoid last-minute frenzy they advise completing all physical preparations, such as packing a first-aid kit, well beforehand.

I can picture myself laid up in some hotel room while my mother does Adventureland with my daughter. I cram my suitcase full of Tylenol, Gravol, Valium, decongestants, antihistamines, laxatives, and herbal remedies for everything from ptomaine poisoning to aging until there's no room left for my clothes.

I repack the Gravol in my carryon. My daughter always

needs it — the minute we leave to go on vacation she throws up in anticipation of the excitement of getting home. I'm taking extra-strength Tylenols for my mother also, in case she's put her back out. She's been lifting weights to get in shape for the holiday (she spent all winter assembling the "right" wardrobe and now has to lose weight to fit into it), attending Jazzercize, and walking ten miles a day. "We're not assaulting Everest," I remind her as she massages her calves all the way to the airport. "We're going to Disneyland."

"Touch wood," she replies. She has been doing some prevacation research also and has become an expert on jet plane crashes, dividing them by aircraft type, location, airline, and number of corpses. And what of the aircraft we're about to entrust our lives to? "This one *always* crashes," she reassures me after we've cleared security.

In the departure lounge each of us has a last-minute "Terror of the Moment Before." My daughter has forgotten to feed her gobies; my mother can't remember if she turned off the back burner on the stove. I phone home to remind my husband to claim the $300,000 flight insurance I'm entitled to "if the plane crashes. And my organ-donor card is with my life insurance policy in my safety deposit —"

"And the key to your safety deposit box is in the black box with your will in the top drawer of your filing cabinet," my husband finishes for me. "Have a wonderful trip!"

"And don't forget to feed the fish!"

The three of us are beyond tears by the time we get our seat belts fastened. We take off over Pat Bay, then my daughter spots our house! It has, from the air, a haunted look. It helps when I think of the home improvements my husband will be able to make with $300,000.

As the plane reaches cruising altitude, my daughter reaches for the motion sickness bag, which *she* calls her homesickness bag. It's the sign I've been waiting for. We're on vacation.

Susan Musgrave

THE TIME OF OUR LIVES

❉ "Whooooaaaa, little dawgie!" comes the captain's voice as the plane digs its tires into hot tarmac at John Wayne Airport. He wishes us all a "safe stay in Los Angeles."

My mother clutches *Security Tips for the Vacation Traveller*. For my holiday reading I'd chosen Ian McEwan's *The Child in Time*, and I'd just reached the part where the father turns his back on his shopping cart to pick out some oranges and his daughter is kidnapped. In the crowded baggage area I grip my daughter's hand.

My mother has forgotten the aliases she used on each of her suitcases ("Don't use tags which indicate correct name and address of residence to be left vacant," warns *Security Tips*), so we use most of the afternoon identifying her Samsonite. To pass the time waiting in line at the taxi stand, I memorize the face on the posters asking HAVE YOU SEEN THIS CHILD?

I hug my daughter so hard she says it hurts, but I don't let up until we're safe inside a cab. My mother, conducting a futile search for seat belts, finds the bullet holes in her door.

"Ventilation," explains our driver, who is missing an eye. He has LOVE tattooed across the knuckles of his deformed hand, and HATE across his good one. "Where to, ladies?"

My mother doesn't answer. She has her book open again, and I follow her eyes over the paragraph beginning "Let someone that can be trusted know your destination."

"The Anaheim area," I answer for her. Our driver starts us on a cross-country tour of six express lanes, while my daughter explains that my mother is having culture shock. The city where we live would fit inside the airport parking lot.

"It's easy to disappear in this town," the cabbie agrees, his lost eye holding us hostage in the rearview mirror.

"Disneyland Hotel," says my mother.

After spending the rest of the afternoon in the lobby arguing ("Don't accept a room which is located on the first floor."), my daughter wants to check out the pool. My mother needs a nap; I bolt the door, close the blinds, and return to *The Child in Time*. When I reach the part where the father sticks MISSING posters in all the shop windows, I drop the book. My Lolita would be impossible to miss, with her waist-length golden hair, nymphlike body, and Day-Glo two-piece bathing suit. I bolt for the pool.

The next day my daughter doesn't want to go anywhere. In one way I'm relieved: it would be safer to spend our vacation locked in our hotel room. On the other hand, my mother would be disappointed if we didn't see Disneyland. In the end a bribe works: if my daughter comes with us, I'll rent *Honey, I Shrunk the Kids*.

"You're the one who *really* wants to go to Disneyland," she accuses me as I buy three-day passes at the gate.

"She's right," says my mother, who snaps me shaking Goofy's paw by a souvenir stand in Fantasyland. "When you were her age, you used to *beg* us to bring you here."

Back then I was innocent. Now I know too much. Hurtling through Space Mountain, I recall that "approximately 150,000 individual pieces are replaced annually at Disneyland," and I spend the entire subterranean cruise through Pirates of the Caribbean panicking about earthquakes. After passing Peter Pan's Lost Boys and Girls Information booth one time too many, I purchase a pair of handcuffs in Frontierland. For the rest of our holiday my daughter and I are inseparable.

On our last day my mother suggests we do something completely different. ("Don't establish routine patterns in daily activities," *Security Tips* advises) She uses the morning to lie by the pool getting sunstroke. I finish my book (the child is forever lost) and spend the afternoon desperately seeking bookstores in the Orange County Yellow Pages. When I can't find anything to read (there are more ads for bail bonds than there are bookstores) and my daughter can't find a video she hasn't seen, we buy postcards to send home to make our friends envy us.

Susan Musgrave

But it's not until we're homeward-bound, forty-fifth in line for takeoff due to a near collision in heavy smog, that I truly begin to relax. I'm waving goodbye to the "Happiest Place on Earth" when I feel something tugging at my other sleeve.

"It's about these handcuffs, Mum . . ."

TO THE OUTHOUSE

�֎ "Technology is a way of organizing the universe so that man doesn't have to experience it," said Max Frisch.

For a week my universe has been a cabin on the Queen Charlotte Islands. Without electricity, hot or cold or even running water, telephone, and fax, my life has become unorganized to the point where I'm experiencing every minute of it.

I need to find out the time. My watch stopped the day I arrived and I've a plane to catch in the morning. I have to make my own way to the airport — my friend took her car to a mechanic seven years ago and hasn't got it back yet.

The only paper I've seen all week — we used it to light a fire earlier — was dated December 11, 1983. The news hasn't changed much. "Another hundred people died today . . ." begins our only link with the outside — the CBC — at the top of some unidentified hour. Helen adds an armload of wet cedar to the stove as the newscast concludes with a storm warning.

When there's no news of the time, I tune out and pick up a library book stamped DISCARDED. The title seems apropos. From where I'm sitting — on a cedar stump in thermal underwear, drinking cold nettle tea from a mason jar — I'll no doubt relate meaningfully to *The Frontier Experience*.

I spike my tea with a shot of Jameson's. "There is something in the nature of man which has kept him seeking in this country the new Eden," writes Jack Hodgins in his introduction to the text. A writer, he says, attempts to find some kind of meaning in this search. When he leaves society and journeys "deeper into the forest," always he discovers unknown forces that bend his attention back, inevitably, on himself.

I take the whiskey with me when I have to journey deeper into the forest myself. "Time is nature's way of keeping everything from happening at once," I find carved in the outhouse door. I leave armed with that bit of wisdom and an extra roll of toilet paper to hurl at the black bear — in case I meet him — who broke into Helen's cabin and tried to silence her one concession to technology — the radio. Helen thinks the CBC hurts his ears.

A Lewis Grizzard melody, "When My Love Comes Back from the Ladies' Room Will I Be Too Old to Care?" hurts *my* ears as I make my way back from the outhouse. We sit up getting drunker while the night grows old. If the CBC *ever* tells us the time, by then it will be too late to matter.

The door is barricaded against the bear. We're down to the last dregs of whiskey, and the only bootlegger on the island is drying out on the mainland. There's nothing left to do but finish *The Frontier Experience.* On the last page I find some exercises, such as "Write a short passage, in prose or poetry, expressing your feelings when completely alone."

I could write volumes. I must have fallen asleep plotting, for the next thing I know I'm being awakened by *Morningside*, playing "Time after Time" and an empty whiskey bottle being hurled at the door. Helen switches off the radio; the bear leaves. "See?" she says to me.

It's still raining as we make our goodbyes and I hike the mile out to the road. The first fisherman to come by in a half ton stops. I settle into a pile of gill nets, then ask if he has a watch.

"I had a digital," he tells me, "but I lost it in the winch." He shows me an empty sleeve.

We drive on in silence. Closer to the airport the fisherman pulls over for an old man hauling a suitcase behind him. We offer the old man a ride. "No thanks," he replies. "I'm in a hurry."

I make it to the airport just in time, as far as I can tell. The hour hand on the waiting room clock dropped off when it was being installed. A replacement has been on order since time immemorial.

I board as the last call for passengers travelling on Time Air's connector flight to Vancouver is being announced. Waiting for takeoff, the flight attendant offers a newspaper to the old man — the one who was in a hurry — seated in front of me.

"Is it today's?" he asks her.

She gives him a puzzled look. "Of course it is. This is the twentieth century, sir."

I adjust my watch. It's not the precise time, but it's a beginning.

BITE DOWN HARD

❉ "All this fuss about sleeping together," says Evelyn Waugh. "For physical pleasure I'd sooner go to my dentist any day." Personally I would rather give my eyeteeth than open wide for a dentist's drill, but I've ignored *this* toothache too long.

Pliny recommends sprinkling the ashes of a mad dog's skull in your ear as a cure, but a mad dog is hard to find. I try deep breathing and oil of cloves, but all I get is light-headed and a bad taste in my mouth. I make the appointment.

"Scared of the Dentist's Chair?" is the feature article in the magazine I bring with me from the waiting room. "Your fears may be justified. . . . but not for the reasons you'd expect," I read as a dental assistant swings the tray into position so I can't escape. She tilts the chair back until the soles of my feet are parallel to the ceiling; the blood drains to my head, and I break into a cold sweat at the next line: "Human beings are being transformed into walking time bombs by having the toxic metal mercury put into their mouths." I'm gnashing the inside of my mouth the way I do when I'm working on a poem.

"Now I recognize your face!" says the assistant, wiping spit from the corners of my mouth. "I saw your picture in *People* magazine!"

It was a local weekly giveaway, but I don't want to disillusion her. I remember her, too: we went to high school together. She was one of the chosen ones with straight pearly whites who made the cheerleading team. Kathy wouldn't remember me, though. While she shook her pom-poms and did the splits, I lurked under the bleachers, writing couplets dedicated to Count Dracula and daydreaming abut having my crooked teeth filed into points. While she won the affections of the football team, I won a prize for my poem about a spinster visiting her cat's grave by moonlight — a copy of Shakespeare's *Much Ado About Nothing.*

One line from the play has stayed with me. "For there was never yet philosopher / That could endure the toothache patiently," says Leonato. I've almost decided that I'm not the sort of patient to endure, when Dr. Harper arrives, pulling on his surgical gloves. "Written any good books lately?" he inquires. Before I can think of an answer he adds, "Bite down hard. Now open up. *You* still have a chewing habit."

If my mouth wasn't full of his nicotine-stained fingers, I would tell him that chewing is an occupational habit. One writer I know used to spit blood in the sink each morning after pulverizing the inside of his mouth while dreaming he had misplaced a comma in his writing, throwing off the speech pattern he gave to a character who lived two hundred years ago.

"Any history of mental illness?" Dr. Harper asks, still probing. The mentally ill often exhibit similar advanced molar grindings, he explains. "Or it could be you clench your teeth when you write."

Dr. Harper, when he first learned I was a poet, discussed

Solyman Brown's *Dentologia: A Poem on Diseases of the Teeth in Five Cantos* as he searched my mouth for "Public Enemy Number One" (tartar). I've since found out he has literary opinions on everything. "James Joyce wrote *Ulysses* when he was suffering from toothache; you should be able to have one cavity drilled without freezing," he informs me today.

I don't see the connection, but it's hard to argue with a guy who can shove a rubber dam into your mouth. And staring up into Dr. Harper's nose hairs, I think of a short story by Bronwen Wallace — a father insists his daughters have their teeth filled without freezing. "'What kind of mothers will you be,' he once asked, 'if you can't take a little pain?'"

"If it hurts, just make a sign," Dr. Harper says, revving his high-speed drill.

"Think philosophically," says Kathy. "Before you know it, it'll all be over."

With the amount of toxic mercury about to be deposited in my mouth, I fear it is my *life* that will soon be over. I taste my own blood as my inquisitor begins anew.

"Sold any of your books to the movies lately?" he asks as Kathy passes him more gleaming hardware. "Open wide, that's it. When I retire, *I'm* going to write a book. Tell me, does it help to get published if you know somebody?"

I can't help myself. I bite down, hard.

INVENTING IN DESPERATE SITUATIONS

❊ The wealthy parents of a young poet complained to me that their "genius" had left her American Express card behind when she went travelling. "She's hitchhiking through Europe, sleeping in ditches — *on purpose!*"

Suffering is one of the main conditions of artistic experience, I reassure them. I've spent a few nights in ditches myself; I've also travelled in "style." But all a gold card ever did was insulate me from the excruciating nausea of being.

There must be some poets, the parents argue, who live comfortably and are still able to write. Dorothy Parker made the same argument: "Living in a garret doesn't get you anywhere unless you're some sort of a Keats," she said. Parker claimed to have known plenty of writers in the twenties who were able to find stories and novels, and good ones, in conflicts that came out of two million dollars a year, not a garret.

As a poet, I've never known the angst of having too much money, or security. "Fear ringed by doubt is my eternal moon," as Malcolm Lowry said. But what about poets who *are* privileged? Does it make facing that blank paper any less crummy on the nerves?

Anne Wilkinson, who died thirty years ago, was raised in a privileged Ontario enclave. The poet grew up in her grandfather's Toronto mansion, Craigleigh. On matters of manners her nurse consulted *Inquire Within Upon Everything;* one line on the deportment of ladies stayed with Wilkinson for life: "If her teeth be good, she should smile but seldom, if bad, not at all."

Eccentricity, in Wilkinson's world, was taken for granted (her family played bridge at a card table set up in the back of their car as they rolled through the streets of Toronto), although private emotions were seldom granted expression. There was another price to be paid for a sheltered life in a home with "eternal rooms" and Raeburns on every wall: safety and closure are not places of adventure, or experience.

There was little in my childhood to stop life from being suffered directly. Our cottage was nicknamed after a Grimm's tale — "The Vinegar Jug." It had four rooms, and rats in the walls. I never had my teeth straightened because my parents thought a crooked smile would build character. The family car had two doors that wouldn't open; you entered through the windows that wouldn't close. Private emotions, in my family, were expressed frequently.

But neither a privileged upbringing nor a humble one prepares any woman writer for the ultimate in human suffering: motherhood. As mothers we make an unspoken promise to our offspring at birth: that we will match their capacity to inflict suffering with our capacity to endure.

"Being a poet and being a mother both need a lot of getting away from," Wilkinson wrote in her journal after her marriage to a prominent surgeon and the birth of her youngest child when she was thirty years old and beginning to write seriously. In one of her best-known poems, "Lens," Wilkinson projects a double self-image: her "woman's eye is weak / And veiled with milk" while her poet's eye is "crystal" and "muscled / With a curious tension." "Though the demands of motherhood created a divided personality," Joan Coldwell writes in her introduction to a new collection of Wilkinson's poetry — and a prose memoir — ('Exile Press'), "the eye/I is not so divided as the poem's contrasts seem to suggest, for the terms used of the poet's tasks are those usually associated with the housewife's. 'daily chore,' 'keep and cherish,' 'polished.' Privileged or not, Wilkinson was, like many woman writers, by nature of her gender, oppressed. As Adrienne Rich, the poet renowned for *Of Woman Born*, has noted, "Those who speak largely of the human condition are usually those most exempt from its oppression — whether of sex, race, or servitude."

"So poets have to suffer in order to write?" ask the long-suffering parents of the genius sleeping in ditches.

I'd recommend it. Poets often have to sink to a level of desperation before they find the poem inside them they can write. Jean-Paul Sartre said genius is not a gift, but rather the way one invents in desperate situations.

But my own sleepless nights are over; now I pass out on a

queen-size bed. I no longer need to suffer for experience's sake. When I *really* want to suffer, I write.

THE DISPENSER OF INVENTION

❋ When Mgungu Yabba Mgungu, the purple-skinned people eater of Tama Janowitz's novel, *A Cannibal in Manhattan,* is transported from his South Sea island to the Big Apple, he visits the Museum of Primitive Cultures. As he peers into the glass cabinets filled with glittering trinkets, voodoo kits, and bone carvings, he concludes, "It was uncivilized and brutal stuff and it was a sorry sight to see how low man could sink before moving up."

All objects created by a culture give clues about a particular way of life. Imagine, a few centuries from now, some culture-hungry tourist visiting the Museum of Modern Man: what would so many uncivilized objects — from plastic doggie-doo to lighted pineapple table centrepieces — say about our society?

Right after Christmas I went to see the manager of a shop specializing in kitsch and high-tech gadgets. I intended to demand refunds for some of my more useless presents — the Dancing Can, for example, that gyrates in time to the coffee grinder.

Harry, who said he couldn't give refunds, suggested I exchange the Talking Dog Leash for Reincat — his hottest seller of the season. I doubt whether Richard Franck had cat antlers in mind when, in 1694, he wrote "Art imitates Nature."

These days art *invents* nature. And Franck, had he been alive today, would not have said "necessity is the mother of invention," either.

I laid my next gift ("you put it in your trunk and close the lid and it looks real," my husband explained when I unwrapped the Surprise Arm and didn't exclaim, "You shouldn't have!") on the counter. Harry thought I might get more pleasure out of a pair of Love Gloves that a couple can snuggle into. My Mood Ring (another gift from my husband — "so you'll know when you have PMS") started turning black.

But while Harry calculated how much I had coming back to me, I saw my chance for revenge: my husband had a birthday coming up. I scooped up some realistic rubber vomit, a package of designer garbage bags, and a mirror that laughs when you look in it.

"You're both writers. You'd appreciate this," said Harry when I told him I also wanted something *extra* special for my mate. He reached for what he called the "ultimate agro-releasing toy," a black box labelled "The Final Word."

"You press this little button," he said, demonstrating. The ultimate word was the familiar four-letter one; I traded my Mood Ring for the Love Gloves instead.

By the time I'd exchanged Dancing Can for a pig-shaped cookie jar that grunts, and Surprise Arm for a frog guaranteed to grow to two hundred times its size in water (the perfect snack for my insatiable two-year-old), I, too, was feeling peckish. I'd planned to buy my brother lunch with Harry's refunds, but after all the trade-offs my wallet was still empty.

My brother, who'd just flown in from Montreal, was waiting at Pagliacci's. He'd ordered a sublime white wine, which we sipped while exchanging presents. Always the diplomat, my brother said, "You shouldn't have!" when he opened the Inflatable Life-size Moose; the practical one in the family, he gave me a Loonie Bank shaped like the Parliament Buildings.

But the bank reminded me I was broke, and that I didn't have any prospects. I was about to order a half portion of Recession-Proof Lasagna when my brother — not only sensible but sensitive — said he'd spring for the bill.

Later, as we rose to leave, I thrust both hands into my Love Gloves. My brother noticed the poor fit (there was enough room for a ménage à trois), which reminded him of the leopard-skin gloves on my Christmas list. He claimed he'd asked everywhere in Montreal for *des gants de lépreux*, but had no luck. The shop clerks just looked at him askance! Finally, on Christmas Eve, he found a bilingual salesclerk who explained that *des gants de lépreux* meant gloves of leper's skin!

Here was a gimmick to put food on the table. ("The stomach is the dispenser of invention," said Persius Flaccus [A.D. 34–62].) "Leper-Skin Gloves: They drop off by themselves." It was horrible enough, and tasteless enough, and we were bound to gross a fortune if we had them in the malls before next Christmas.

We'd sunk as low as two people could sink, but we sat back down, ordered a gently aggressive Burgundy, and planned our upmarketing strategy.

ONE SUPREME CASE OF ORDINARINESS

✳ To a certain extent all of us are a bit odd. As Edith Sitwell said, "Even ordinariness, carried to a high degree of perfection, becomes eccentricity."

"Now *that's* different," says the CTV producer who has phoned to find out if I'm odd enough to appear on his upcoming show featuring eccentrics. His lineup so far includes a Newfoundlander who can cure hiccups by setting fire to his nightshirt, and a yogi from Manitoba who eats foreign cars. He needs someone from the extreme west "to round things out." He's heard about me.

Any eccentricity on my part would be a supreme case of ordinariness, I say, but this doesn't deter him. "Aside from being ordinary, what else would make people consider you eccentric?"

"There's nothing but normalcy in my life," I insist. My daughter's mouth drops open. I draw my hand across my throat; she gets the message and buttons her lip.

Susan Musgrave

"I've got a husband and two kids. I get up at 7:00 a.m., drop the kids at school, write, take a walk, cook dinner, fall asleep, get up, and do it all over again — no addictions, no scandals, a few friends for potluck on weekends."

"That's so normal it's unusual," says the producer. "Next you'll be telling me you're happily married, too! The last time I saw you on the news, I believe you were saying 'I do' in a maximum-security penitentiary."

I've never liked the telephone much. I wrap the cord around my neck in one gesture, pulling it tight — a signal for my husband to invent an emergency. This time he scribbles Gore Vidal's maxim on a scrap of paper: "Never miss a chance to have sex or appear on television."

But I don't like television much. Compared to his other two guests, I try to persuade the producer, nothing I can do would make the slightest visual impact.

"Didn't you pose nude once for a literary magazine? Of course, we wouldn't ask you to appear naked on television, but maybe we could get you reciting poetry in a body stocking?"

Once is eccentric, I tell him. Twice would be madness.

"That reminds me . . . another question. There was that interview on the radio. Something about insanity. I mean, when you were a lot younger?"

The line between eccentricity and madness has always been blurred, I answer, skirting the question. On one hand, I had an "eccentric" uncle who left instructions in his will to be buried head downward, because "the world was turned topsy-turvy and he wanted to be right at last." Then there was my namesake, Susannah, who wrote poetry and hung her walls with pictures of the furniture she couldn't afford to buy, and was considered mad.

"When the rich are peculiar, it's called eccentricity, but if you're poor and you act a bit strange, you're promptly classed as a loonie," I tell him.

"I hear you," says the producer, and congratulates me for being so honest. He wants to give us both time to think. He'll call *mañana*.

"You're weird, Mum," says my daughter as I unplug the telephone. "If you actually saw yourself on television, you'd see how weird you are."

By noon the next day the producer hasn't called. I prepare a bath, wondering if I came across as *too* ordinary on the phone. Just because I simply hold my breath when I get hiccups, or never developed a craving for foreign cars, it doesn't mean I don't have hidden eccentricities.

By the time I remember to plug the phone back in, and the producer gets through, I'm in the middle of an identity crisis.

"I exaggerated," I say. "I'm really not ordinary." I'm in the midst of telling him how I can scratch the back of my neck with my right toe while standing on my head when he cuts me off.

"Listen, you don't have to be creative. Just be yourself." He proposes to give me a minute and a half of prime time to discuss what's most different about me: my ordinariness.

After it's settled, I ask my husband for his help once more. I lie soaking in my bath of pickle juice (I read somewhere this would preserve my body after I die) and I ask him to list all the ordinary things I do each day.

My husband just rolls his eyes and wrings another pickle.

THE END

<hr>

❋ I'm propped up in bed, adding some final touches to my latest manuscript, when my husband arrives home with a book. It's one I ordered months ago when I was feeling suspiciously healthy — *Symptoms: The Book That Answers the Questions: Am I Sick? Is It Serious? Should I Call My Doctor?*

My husband thinks I'm sick because I have finished another column. Every time I write THE END, he says, I take it literally. "Why don't you start a new column right away," he advises as I sketch a headstone around my name on the most recent one.

When he leaves me to rest in peace, I examine my new "easy-to-use home medical reference." It promises to interpret my body's warning signs and put them in perspective. Each symptom is followed by a multiple choice of ills. My "Headache," for instance, can mean "Stress, Hangover, or Brain Tumour." The "Chest Pains" I've been having could be "Heartburn or Heart Attack," and where my "Loss of Appetite" could be something as trivial as a cold, it might as easily be life-threatening — AIDS or cancer.

Then there's the numbness in my elbow I've been ignoring. I scan the index and find numbness under "Lack of Feeling." In the case of another woman my own age who ignored the same symptom for too long, an X ray revealed a tiny malignant tumour that had settled in her elbow bone. Within weeks the cancer had consumed her brain, liver, and lungs. She died before she could blow the candles out on her thirty-ninth birthday cake.

For my "Sore Throat" the diagnosis was more difficult. A sore throat could mean "any number of things from tonsilitis and gonorrhea, to fish or chicken bone." I hadn't eaten fish or chicken due to my "Loss of Appetite" and I'd had my tonsils out when I was five. That left gonorrhea or "any number of things."

By the time I'd finished looking up the symptoms for any number of things, I had developed "Irregular Heartbeat." I called my doctor for an appointment.

"How do you feel?" she asked after a quick check for vital signs. She had my medical history, as thick as both volumes of *The History of the Decline and Fall of the Roman Empire*, open on her desk.

"Fine." And then I told her about my *lack* of feeling.

Interpreting symptoms is no easy task, says the author of *Symptoms*, because most people don't know what they mean or how to describe them. To prove his point he conducted a quiz in his office. After the initial pro forma "How do you feel?" he invented a symptom, asking several of his patients, "Do you have any gribbling?"

"Only when I walk uphill in the cold weather," said one patient. (He had angina pectoris.) "I used to gribble, but not since I had my prostate fixed," said another. "My husband gribbles, but I don't." (She turned out to be perfectly healthy.)

While waiting for my own doctor to put my symptoms in perspective (she was rereading the history of my decline), I thumbed through the *Ms* magazine I'd picked up in the waiting room. "There are times when you *want* to have a disease," Barbara Ehrenreich writes in an article entitled "Sick Chic." "You *have* symptoms, but you need a label for your ills."

Ehrenreich had symptoms — headache, chest pains, loss of appetite, numbness — but, for the longest time, no label. She'd developed PMVS, a disease where one of the valves in the heart doesn't close properly, although not until the medical profession found a name for it did they begin to take it seriously.

That is, they began to look for it. "And they found it: mostly in women who are thin and fair, and — this is the sad part — mostly in people *who did not have any symptoms* at all."

I'm fair, and fairly thin, but when I suggested to my doctor that I ought to have a test for Prolapsed Mitral Valve System, she pried the magazine out of my hands. I had a cold, she said, and the elbow numbness was a symptom of writer's cramp. Both were temporary conditions.

As I left her office, I felt my heart beating harder than ever. (This, too, I told myself, was only temporary.) For the article in *Ms* had given me a new terror to make myself sick over — the diseases I didn't even *have* symptoms for . . . yet.

Susan Musgrave

In nine days — if I make it — I'll be thirty-nine. Not that I'll have it made in any final sense. As George Burns says, you only have it made if you live to be a hundred, because very few people die past that age.